Religion Versus Science:

Where Both Sides go Wrong in the Great Evolution Debate

Religion Versus Science:

Where Both Sides go Wrong in the Great Evolution Debate

Ron Frost

BOOKS

Winchester, UK
Washington, USA

First published by O-Books, 2011
O-Books is an imprint of John Hunt Publishing Ltd., The Bothy, Deershot Lodge, Park Lane, Ropley, Hants, SO24 0BE, UK
office1@o-books.net
www.o-books.com

For distributor details and how to order please visit the 'Ordering' section on our website.

ISBN: 978 1 84694 358 4

A CIP catalogue record for this book is available from the British Library.

Design: Tom Davies

Printed in the UK by CPI Antony Rowe
Printed in the USA by Offset Paperback Mfrs, Inc

CONTENTS

To all my teachers,
those who taught me the thrill of doing Science
and
those who opened me to the wonders of the Buddhadharma

Preface
How this Book came to be

I never intended to write this book or anything like it. Evolution is not my field of research. I am a rock scientist. I use the compositions of minerals and rocks to determine the conditions under which the rocks have formed and, from that, to infer how geological processes operated in the past. Through outrageous good fortune, I have spent my career at the University of Wyoming. For more than 30 years I have roamed the mountains of Wyoming and studied the rocks that crop out there. Wyoming hosts some of the oldest rocks in the world and, as a result, the study of the geological history of the Earth, between 4000 and 2500 million years ago, became one of my major fields of research. To me, the statements made by the Young-Earth Creationists that the Earth is only 6,000 years old is patently ridiculous. However, that was no reason for me to wade into a debate that is bitter, toxic, and vicious, at least not until a strange incident that occurred one January morning in 2002.

I awoke that morning at 5:00 a.m. What an annoying time to wake up. It was too early to get up and probably too late to get any more deep sleep. I rolled over and slipped into a state where I was not quite awake and yet not fully asleep. I found myself giving a formal talk at the university on the evolution debate. In any setting other than the weird world of dreams, this would be a strange subject for me to speak on, because, as I said, my expertise is not in evolution. In this dream, I pointed out that the Creationists, despite being quite wrong about the young age of the Earth, were raising some very valid points. There is something profoundly disturbing about the way that modern biologists present the phenomenon of life, and particularly evolution. Certainly humans are something more that a sac of chemicals, the only purpose of which is to transport our genes from one generation to the next. Certainly life is not purposeless and meaningless and we didn't arrive on the planet by mistake. These and other thoughts spun through my mind until I opened my eyes again. It was 6:30 a.m., the faintest trace of light was coming in the window, and it was time to get up.

I threw the blankets off, slid my feet out of the bed and onto the floor, and sat up on the edge of the bed. I was about to stand up when a voice inside my head said, 'You should write a book about this.'

I was not particularly surprised to hear this voice appear in my head. It had visited me many times before and usually it had given me cogent advice. In fact, I would say that these occasional visits caused my career as a scientist to thrive. This time I hesitated. I sat there with my bare feet on the cold floor and thought about how much research it would take for me to write a book on evolution and how this was a debate that I didn't particularly want to participate in. The thought that I clearly didn't want to write a book on this subject had barely emerged into my consciousness when the voice answered, 'If you don't do it, who will?'

That settled it. With that, I began a project that consumed six years of my life. Fortunately that disembodied energy, or angel (as Christians would call this disembodied voice), or the drala (as Tibetans would call it) that had encouraged me to begin this project continued to assist me throughout the research and writing of the book.* Suggestions of books I should read as background appeared from everywhere. Friends who had no

* Those of you who are convinced that reality is composed of only the physical world and are offended by this sentence may want to delete it. In its place you may substitute this sentence: 'As I proceeded to work on this project I continually encountered strange occurrences and bizarre coincidences that made the work easier.'

idea I was writing this book would mention a book to me that turned out to be important. Sometimes over breakfast or dinner I would hear the review of a book on National Public Radio that would provide key information to me. I even found a book on the origin of life reviewed in EOS, the weekly paper of the American Geophysical Union, a place where one would hardly expect to find a book on life mentioned. Often, when a problem stumped me, a thought would come to me that I should check the library catalogue or the web for some subject. Sure enough, more times than not, there lay the answer I needed.

The most memorable incident occurred in winter of 2003. I was writing Chapter 10 (the chapter summarizing evolution) and needed to find out when the first vertebrates (or chordates) appeared in the geologic record. I went to the Geology Library and I remember surveying the many shelves of books on paleontology. Where was I to start? It could take hours for me to find the answer I needed to write a sentence or, at most, a paragraph in my book. I grabbed a book randomly off a shelf, opened it in a random place, and there before me was a section summarizing the evolutionary history of chordates. In a few moments I had written the section of the text I needed.

As I wrote the book, the text often flowed effortlessly into the computer. Many times, after I finished my evening's work, I would read over what I had written and it would seem as if I had just read it for the first time. I would often remark to my self, 'Wow! This is well written,' and I would wonder how it was that I had come up with such fine analogies or images; I certainly didn't remember struggling to write them down.

Finally in early 2004 I had finished the first draft of the book and began to look for a publisher. I thought this would be an easy job, because my book was taking a stand in the middle ground on a major social issue. At first I tried marketing the book myself to publishers of spiritual books. When this lead to no success I started looking for an agent. The search stretched on for more than four years, during which time I learned far more than I cared to know about the publishing industry. In April 2008 I sent a query to the agent Krista Goering. Over the next few months I sent her, first, a proposal and sample chapters, and then the whole text. Finally, in mid-August, I received a very polite rejection from her. She liked the book but simply didn't know where to place it. Although it was one the nicest rejections I have ever received, it was still a rejection, my 109th. Two days later, before I had time to send out a letter of inquiry to yet another agent, I received another e-mail from Krista. In it she said that she had received a query from a publisher named John Hunt looking for manuscripts relating to science and religion. She asked me if she could send him my proposal. Within five days I had an agent and a book contract.

Acknowledgements

This book would never have materialized without the help of many of my friends. Foremost among these is Jeff Lockwood, University of Wyoming's entomologist-turned-philosopher. Jeff read many versions of this manuscript and suggested many ways that the text could be improved. More importantly Jeff was a great source of moral support at the time when it seemed that I would never find a publisher for this work. I also want to thank the three paleontologists from the University of Wyoming, Don Boyd, Jay Lilligraven, and Mark Clementz. They helped me with questions paleontological and read the text to make sure it was P.C. (paleontologically correct). I must admit, however, that they didn't all agree with the conclusions I have drawn, but they were very polite with their criticism on this point. Many other friends read the manuscript and provided me with important suggestions and advice. This includes Bevan Frost and Leila Bruno who provided me with key comments about mistakes in the text and suggestions about how it could be improved. I also want to thank Brendon Orr who helped me with the construction of my website.

Laramie, WY
July 18, 2009

Acknowledgements

[illegible]

PART I

STATEMENT OF THE PROBLEM

Chapter 1
Introduction

Many years ago, a group of blind men lived in an Indian village. Every day they gathered in the shade of the giant trees in the village square, where they held heated discussions on matters philosophical. One day, in an attempt to acquaint these men with the natural world, a mahout brought his elephant over to them. Excitedly the men gathered around it. One fingered the elephant's massive trunk, another felt its broad side, another ran his hands around its enormous feet, and the fourth stroked its smooth, gleaming tusks.
After the mahout left with his elephant, the four men returned to the shade in the square and debated the question: 'What is an elephant?'
One maintained: 'It is like a huge snake.'
'No, it is broad and wide like a wall,' another replied
'You are both wrong,' a third stated, 'it is solid and round like a tree stump.'
'You are all mistaken,' the fourth contended, 'unlike any other beast, it is hard and smooth, like a polished beam of wood.'
For many years thereafter, whenever the men gathered together, the topic of their discussion frequently gravitated toward their debate about the nature of the elephant. Though they argued for many years, they never found an answer to this question.
Ancient Indian Parable

The publication of Charles Darwin's book, *Origin of the Species by Means of Natural Selection,* in November of 1859, marks one of the great events in the history of science. Prior to this, a few naturalists had postulated that species may have changed over time, but until the publication of Darwin's book, the concept of evolution clearly occupied the scientific fringe. Before 1859 most biologists still clung solidly to the literal interpretation of the

Bible and believed that the variety of life seen on Earth is precisely the same as that which decorated the planet at the time of its creation. Darwin's book created a revolution not only because it produced clear evidence that species had changed, but also because it provided biologists with an explanation of how this change occurred.

A storm of controversy greeted the publication of the *Origin of the Species*. Many naturalists embraced the theory immediately, but a considerable number of them refused to accept it. Despite this opposition, the theory of evolution quickly took over as the dominant view of biology and it is the paradigm that governs the science today. Darwin's theory of evolution became one of the first building blocks in the foundation of modern biology. The evidence uncovered by scientists over the past century-and-a-half has only served to strengthen the theory. By the turn of the twentieth century, the growing science of genetics, based in part on Gregor Mendel's work on inheritance in peas, began to explain how adaptive traits within a species could be transferred from one generation to another. In the early decades of the twentieth century, geochemists used radioactive decay to show that the Earth is thousands of millions of years old, which demonstrated that there was plenty of time available for natural selection to produce the variety of life we see today. Finally, in the 1950s biologists unraveled the structure of DNA and RNA, providing us with an understanding of how genetic information is transferred from one generation to another.

In the 150 years since the publication of Darwin's book, every discovery in the fields of biology, biochemistry, geology and cosmology has reinforced the theory of evolution. Despite this, a large proportion of American Christians (and even some American Presidents!) still dispute the veracity of evolution. For more than 80 years, Fundamentalist Christians have had a rather dubious history of trying to restrict the teaching of evolution in our schools. In 1925 the legislature of the state of Tennessee passed a law forbidding the teaching of evolution. With the backing of the ACLU, John Scopes, a young science teacher in Dayton, Tennessee, flouted this law, thus allowing himself to be prosecuted. The resulting Scopes trial became a national spectacle known as the 'Monkey Trial'. Although the trial involved a number of complex social issues in addition to the teaching of evolution, it is commonly portrayed as the opening shot in the battle between Darwinism and religion in America. The well-known lawyer, Clarence Darrow, defended Scopes, and William Jennings Bryan, a three-time presidential candidate, led the prosecution. Scopes lost the trial and was fined $100, but higher courts overturned the verdict on a technicality. The ridicule heaped upon the state of Tennessee during the 'Monkey Trial' caused many other states to shelve similar laws, or at least not to prosecute teachers who violated them. Even so, the Tennessee law against teaching evolution and similar laws in Mississippi and Arkansas remained on the books until 1968, when they were finally declared unconstitutional by the United States Supreme Court.

The Supreme Court ruling of 1968, however, did not solve the matter. In response to the conservative revival during the late 1970s, America saw a renewal in the fundamentalist's resistance to the theory of evolution. A new field of study emerged, calling itself Creation Science. It claimed to prove the Biblical story of creation using scientific reasoning. Throughout the 1980s, Creationists, headed by Henry Morris, published a number of books on Creation Science.[1] In response to these books scientists produced a spate of papers and books arguing that there is no scientific basis to Creationism.[2] In 1981, both Alabama and Louisiana passed laws requiring the schools to teach Creationism along with evolution. The Creationists fared very badly in the lawsuits that arose in response to these laws. Scientists shredded the arguments that Creation Science was 'scientific' and the courts ruled that these laws were unconstitutional because

Creationism is thinly disguised Fundamentalist Christian religion.

The legal losses did not slow the opponents to evolution. First, they changed their approach to make it appear less overtly driven by a literal interpretation of the Bible. In 1991, Phillip Johnson introduced an attack on Darwinism that he called 'Intelligent Design'. The advocates of Intelligent Design maintain that the biochemical processes of life are so complex that they could not have arisen spontaneously, as evolutionists imply. They also contend that, whereas small degrees of change may occur within species, there is no evidence that evolution causes the appearance of a new species.[3] As a result, they conclude that there must have been a Creator for all we see in nature. Second, opponents of evolution also changed their tactics; they turned away from using legislation to force the teaching of Creationism and began to establish these regulations through control of state and local boards of education.

In 1999, the Kansas state board of education made the teaching of evolution in schools voluntary. The backlash to this decision followed quickly. In the 2000 elections, all the members of the board of education who supported that ruling were voted out of office. Very shortly thereafter the Kansas board of education rescinded the ruling. The battle, however, was far from over. In 2004, the anti-evolution forces gained control of the Kansas school board again and in 2005 introduced new regulations regarding teaching evolution. Not only did the board put forth a proposal requiring teaching alternate views to evolution, but even redefined science as the philosophy of naturalism (as opposed to a process of studying the natural world).[4] The pro-science forces regained control of the school board in the 2006 elections, which kept the teaching of science unsullied in Kansas.

In 2002, the advocates of Intelligent Design presented the Ohio board of education with a proposal to require teaching Intelligent Design along with evolution. After a long and rancorous debate, the ID proposal was defeated. In the summer of 2005, the board of education of Dover, Pennsylvania passed rules allowing the teaching of Intelligent Design in science classrooms. In December of 2005, Federal Judge John E. Jones III ruled that ID, like Creation Science, was only thinly veiled Fundamentalist Christian theology and that teaching ID in science classes was unconstitutional. This decision, however, has done little to deter the advocates of Intelligent Design who are clamoring in school boards throughout the country that evolution be taught as 'merely a theory'. Yet again, the scientific community is rallying to defend itself against a movement that is trying to force a religious position into the science curriculum that would compromise the scientific method.[5]

Why is there such a strong resistance to the theory of evolution among a certain population of Americans? Why do new attempts to weaken the teaching of evolution arise hydra-like whenever an old proposal has been struck down? Are Creationists and proponents of Intelligent Design irrational anti-intellectuals who are desperately trying to hold back the progress of knowledge, or is there more to the story? Could it be that this dispute has endured for nearly 150 years because the groups arguing each side of the question, like the blind men in the Indian parable quoted at the beginning of this chapter, have only a partial view of reality, making it impossible to find common ground between them? These are some of the questions I will explore in this book.

Chapter 2
A brief history

To understand the elements behind the great debate between Darwinism and Creationism we must start with a brief summary of the history of Western Society since the Renaissance. The many forces that were released by this social explosion are still reverberating through society and are intimately entwined within the debate.

For more than a thousand years before the sixteenth century, the work of two Greek philosophers, Aristotle and Ptolemy, dominated science (or natural philosophy as it was then known). Aristotle, who lived in the fourth century BCE, was one of the first philosophers to classify the natural world. As the world's first biologist, he catalogued the species that he found around him. Although he believed that life could generate spontaneously from non-living material, he maintained that the species themselves were unchanging. He also stated that the Earth was the center of the universe, while the moon, sun and other celestial bodies circulated around it, beneath an enclosing sphere that contained the stars. He thought that the celestial bodies were perfect and unchanging. Only the Earth was subject to change, which was seen in the progression of the seasons and the birth and death of all beings on the planet. All impermanent celestial phenomena, such as rainbows, meteors, and comets, occurred in the space between the Earth and the Moon.

In the second century C.E. Ptolemy modified the Aristotelian model to explain better the orbits of the planets as observed from Earth. In this model, Earth is located in the center of the solar system and the moon, sun, and planets occupy hollow spheres revolving around it. It is easy to understand how the sun and the moon fit into this model because we see them rise in the east and set in the west with a distinct periodicity. However, it is more difficult to see how this model explains the orbits of the planets because sometimes they appear to be moving in the reverse direction against the starry background. To account for this, Ptolemy postulated that the planets were revolving on spheres that are nested within a larger sphere, which marks their orbit around the Earth. Ptolemaic theory predicted the path of the planets so well that it remained undisputed for more than a thousand years.

In the thirteenth century, the Catholic theologian, Thomas Aquinas, incorporated the Aristotelian and Ptolemaic models of nature and the cosmos into his comprehensive philosophy of the world. This made the teachings of Aristotle and Ptolemy an aspect of the Catholic Church's dogma, a move that had an important impact three centuries later when the nascent realm of science began to question the veracity of the classical view of the world.

If you were living in Europe in the early years of the sixteenth century, you would have grown up in a society with the following view of reality: the Earth stood in the center of creation with the sun, moon, and planets rotating around it. In addition, the cosmos had a distinct history. It began with creation, evolved through the fall, the expulsion of Adam and Eve from Eden, and continued to the crucifixion and resurrection of Jesus, who promised the redemption of humanity. Finally, the universe would come to an end at some time in the not-too-distant future with the Last Judgment. This was a very comfortable cosmology for, with man the most important creature on Earth, and Earth in the center of the universe, it was clear that the universe revolved around us. This fit nicely with the Biblical concept that man was created in God's image and that the Earth was placed here for human use and care.

The first hint of trouble with this beautiful picture came in 1543 with the publication of the book *Revolution of Celestial Bodies* by Nicholas Copernicus, which stated that the sun, not the Earth, lay in the center of the solar system. Copernicus' model nicely explained the observed velocities of the planets, with the fastest planet, Mercury, lying closest to the sun and the slowest, Saturn, being furthest (the outermost planets of the solar system, Uranus, Neptune and little Pluto, of course, at that time were unknown). However, it meant that the Earth was flying through space at the speed of the other planets, something that seemed totally illogical. Furthermore, somehow the Earth managed to bring its moon along with it. Because of these problems, and because there was no direct evidence that could distinguish between Copernicus' and Ptolemy's models of the universe, the two views existed side by side for more than a century.

Initially, the heliocentric view of the solar system had few adherents, but as the sixteenth century wore on, scientists made more discoveries that questioned the veracity of the Aristotelian and Ptolemaic view of the universe. In November 1572, a new star, something we would now call a supernova, arose in the northern sky and in autumn 1577 a great comet appeared. By the use of parallax, the Danish Astronomer Tycho Brahe showed that both of these features lay far beyond the moon, challenging the Aristotelian concept that the heavens are immutable. Another blow came in 1609, when the German astronomer Johannes Kepler demonstrated that the orbits of the planets around the sun were elliptical, not circular. This was important because the circle is a perfect figure and, according to the Classical view of astronomy, the perfect celestial bodies moved in perfect circles. The ellipse is not a perfect figure like the circle, so Kepler's observation was a major attack on the very concept that the motion of the stars reveals the actions of the gods, an underpinning to the study of astronomy since the days of the early Greeks.

In 1608, the Italian mathematician Galileo Galilei aimed a telescope, which had recently been invented, at the skies and in 1610 he described his observations in a book called *Starry*

Messenger. He found that the objects of the heavens were not the perfect celestial spheres as postulated by Aristotle and Ptolemy. Numerous craters pockmarked the surface of the moon and dark blemishes seemed to move across the surface of the sun. He also noted that four moons orbited Jupiter. This was a shocking discovery because both the Ptolemaic and Copernican models noted that Jupiter moved through the heavens. If Jupiter could move through space and bring its moons with it, why couldn't the Earth do the same? Finally Galileo trained his telescope on Venus and recorded that it showed phases like the moon. In the Ptolemaic model, Venus revolved in a circle between the sun and the Earth. In this configuration, an observer from Earth could never see a fully illuminated face of Venus. Only if Earth and Venus both revolved around the sun could an observer on Earth see all the phases of Venus.

Galileo's book had immediate impact on the debate over the Ptolemaic and Copernican models of the solar system. In 1616, in an effort to suppress the growing popularity of the heliocentric view of the solar system, the Inquisition placed Copernicus' book, *Revolution of Celestial Bodies,* on the *Index of Prohibited Books.* At the same time, the Vatican cautioned Galileo to stop teaching the Copernican theory. When, in 1623, a new pope, Urban IV, took office, Galileo gained permission to publish his book, *Dialogue Concerning the Two Chief World Systems,* which finally appeared in 1632. In this book, three characters debated the validity of the Ptolemaic and Copernican theories. Galileo had cleverly set up the format of the book so that the authorities could not say that he was 'teaching' heliocentrism. However, the book treated the views of the Church with derision, even to the point of naming the character arguing the geocentric view Simplico, or 'simpleton'. The Vatican responded to this insult with fury. In February 1633, they called Galileo before the Inquisition. The case involved far more than mere heresy; for there was also a question as to whether Galileo had violated the oath he took in

1616 not to teach about a mobile Earth. As a result of this trial, the Vatican banned Galileo's book, forced Galileo under the threat of torture to sign a statement that he no longer believed that the Earth revolved around the sun, and put him under house arrest for the rest of his life.

The Catholic Church's prosecution of Galileo had two long-term effects. First, it drove the center of intellectual inquiry away from the Mediterranean to Northern Europe, where the Protestant revolution had destroyed the influence of the Catholic Church. The Protestant churches were no friendlier toward science than was the Vatican. However, the clergy did not control the state in the north, as they did in the Catholic countries, and hence they could not stop scientific inquiry. It was in the north that the English genius, Sir Isaac Newton, published his book *Principia Mathematica* in 1687, which described the laws of gravity. This explained how the planets revolved around the sun without flying into space, why the orbits were elliptical, and how the Earth could bring its moon with it as it circled the sun. Newton's discovery of the gravitational laws heralded the final demise of the Ptolemaic view of the universe.

The second effect of the persecution of Galileo was far more profound; it set the stage for the great battle between science and religion, which continues to this day. By attacking Galileo so viciously, the clerics in the Vatican established in the minds of many in Western society that the forces of science were forward-looking and progressive whereas religion consisted of close-minded reactionaries. The many battles that were fought subsequently between the Church and the rational worldview only served to reinforced this view. These battles included not only conflicts between the growing fields of science and the stolid dogmatism of the Church, but also the political struggles between democracy and church-supported monarchies.

One of the final blows in this long struggle came in 1859 with the publication of Darwin's *The Origin of the Species.* In this book,

Darwin noted that the Earth has limited resources. As a result, only the strongest and best-fit individuals of each species could succeed in the struggle to survive. Over time, this process of natural selection will make individuals of each species adapt to their environment. Darwin also postulated that natural selection is the process that allows species to change through time. The development of Darwinism was the final step in the dismantling of the medieval cosmology. Naturally, many Christians responded to Darwin's theory with dismay, but by the middle of the nineteenth century the Church's influence over Western Society had diminished to such an extent that there was little they could do but to raise impotent protests.

The Rise of Materialism

Needless to say, the scientific revolution has had a profound effect on Western Society. Our lifestyle today is far more comfortable than what could be imagined by people living even 100 years ago. We can travel nearly anywhere on the globe in a matter of hours, we can communicate with friends around the world with a click of a computer key, and we have access to medical technologies that are nothing short of amazing. The scientific revolution raised our standard of living so dramatically that it has had a major impact on our culture. Because of the profound changes that science has brought to the world, our society views becoming a scientist as one of the most important intellectual endeavors one can pursue.

Science is the study of the material world, and as a result, gradually, many people in Western Society came to believe that only the material aspect of reality is important. At the same time, many people in Western Society, especially scientists, relegate religion, which is the study of the transcendental aspects that lie beyond the material world, to the dustbin of history. This attitude toward religion is not only a response to the reactionary image that religion earned in its battle against scientific progress; it also arises because scientific studies seem to have a direct effect in advancing human knowledge, something that appears to be lacking in religious studies.

It is difficult for us, who are immersed in modern society, to appreciate how different the scientific view of reality is from that which came before. Before the scientific revolution, people attributed all unusual natural phenomena, such as lightning, rainbows, meteorites, or earthquakes, to some supernatural cause. To people living in pre-scientific societies, the world was populated with unseen beings, such as ghosts, pixies, elves and leprechauns, who interacted with humans in strange and often malevolent ways. Over the past five centuries, science has shown that the phenomena in the world around us arise purely from natural causes. These causes can be understood by making careful observations and applying reason to the data that has been collected. As science has come to understand the workings of the natural world, the ghosts, pixies, elves, and leprechauns that seemingly used to populate it have slowly faded away.

This worldview – that all phenomena have a natural, as opposed to a supernatural explanation – is called *naturalism*. To say that a phenomenon happens because God deems it to, immediately closes any intellectual probing into how that phenomenon could have occurred. Science, as we know it, therefore, could not have emerged until a certain portion of society developed a naturalistic view of the world. Empirical science did not develop in the Greek and Roman societies because the ancient philosophers were suspicious of knowledge provided by the senses and believed that only thoughts were truly pure. These philosophers concentrated their efforts on the study of ideas and, though they developed very sophisticated mathematics, their grasp of science remained primitive. Science did not develop in Western Society during the medieval period because the intellectual endeavors at that time concentrated on the world that will come after death and paid little attention to the impure material world. For similar reasons, science and technology remained relatively primitive in Eastern societies, which concentrated mostly on the subjective world of the mind. Thus it was only with the rise of naturalism during the Renaissance that an intellectual climate appeared that could accommodate the birth and development of science.

The version of naturalism that arose during the 16th and 17th centuries was quite content to co-exist with the Christian view of God. It was only later that science developed a strong materialistic ethos. There is a subtle but critical difference between naturalism, as defined above, and materialism, which maintains that the physical world is the **only** reality and that all other aspects of our experience, thoughts, feeling, and emotions, are simply products of physical processes

Table 1
Terms Describing Possible Views of the Natural World

Concept	*Physical phenomena can be ascribed to natural, rather than supernatural processes*	*The physical world is all there is*
Commonly used terms	*Methological Naturalism*	*Ontological Naturalism*
	Scientific Materialism	*Materialism*
Term used in this book	*Naturalism*	*Materialism*

Unfortunately, in modern usage, the terms 'materialism' and 'naturalism' are often considered synonymous, and this has lead to considerable confusion. To clear up some of this terminological fuzziness, Robert Pennock distinguished *methodological* naturalism (i.e. naturalism as a method of studying the phenomenal world), which carries no implications regarding a transcendent reality from *ontological* naturalism (i.e. naturalism that describes the nature of the phenomenal world), which is synonymous with materialism (Table 1).[6] Another term that is frequently used to describe the scientific view of the world is 'scientific materialism'. Technically, it should be synonymous with 'methodological naturalism'; however, many modern writers use it in an ontological context. To make the terminology in this book as clear as possible, I will restrict the use of the term 'naturalism' to mean methodological naturalism. It will carry no implications about the existence or non-existence of a transcendental being. When I wish to describe the concepts implying that there is nothing to reality but the material world, I will use the term 'materialism' (rather than 'ontological naturalism'). Because of the confusion over the contextual meaning of 'scientific materialism', I shall not use this term at all.

It may seem that I am splitting hairs by spending more than two pages distinguishing between the definitions of 'naturalism' and 'materialism'. However, recognizing the distinction between these definitions is critical to understanding the conflict between science and religion. As noted above, naturalism makes no statement about the existence (or non-existence) of God, whereas materialism is distinctly atheistic. The earliest scientists, such as Newton, did not consider their studies to be antithetical to religion. They were deists who envisioned that God had set the whole universe in motion and then let it run without His intervention. As such, they considered that science was a tool to understand the laws that governed the operation of God's world. Only in the 19th and 20th centuries did the scientific view of the world change from naturalism to materialism. By the end of the 20th Century, only 40% of American scientists (and only 7% of scientists in the National Academy of Sciences) believed in God, compared to 93% of the general population.[7]

It is not surprising that Western Society has become increasingly more materialistic over the past few centuries. Throughout the nineteenth and early twentieth centuries, the material aspects of the world – the steam engines and the fuel that ran them, the steel and the ore from which it was made, and the generators that could produce electricity – all became increasingly more important to modern society. Meanwhile, the spiritual dimension of the world shrank before the illumination of an ever-growing scientific knowledge. As material objects have become more important to the operation of a healthy economy, the spiritual world appeared to become progressively more marginalized.

The worldview of materialism couldn't be further from the view that held sway up to the end of the Middle Ages. Instead of being the center of a universe that God created for our purposes, mankind has been displaced to the periphery of a cold, impersonal universe. As indicated by famous biologist Richard Dawkins, such a universe

> ...would be neither evil nor good in intention. It would manifest no intentions of any kind. In a universe of physical forces and genetic replication, some people are going to get hurt, other people are going to get lucky, and you won't find any rhyme or reason in it, nor any justice. The universe that we observe has precisely the properties we should expect if there is, at bottom, no design, no purpose, no evil and no good, nothing but blind, pitiless indifference.[8]

As grim as this view sounds, it is made worse by the implication that the non-material world of our feelings, emotions, and thoughts, is merely an epiphenomenon of our brain. In this view, our insights, intuition, and creativity are simply products of the chemical and electrical activity going on inside our heads and have little importance or meaning in the larger scale of things. This is well expressed by the Nobel laureate Francis Crick in the first sentence of his book, *The Astonishing Hypothesis:*

> The Astonishing Hypothesis is that 'You', your joys and your sorrows, your memories and your ambitions, your sense of personal identity and free will, are in fact no more than the behavior of a vast assembly of nerve cells and their associated molecules.[9]

In addition to belittling non-objective aspects of human experience, materialism has removed meaning from our existence. As noted by William Provine:

> I see no cosmic or ultimate meaning in human life. The ultimate universe cares nothing for us and will either continue to expand and cool, leading to an extermination of all living creatures in the universe, or will cease to expand and will begin closure, which will result in everything crashing together in an unbelievably small space, thus obliterating all life. Humans are nothing in the evolutionary process of life, and only a few individuals are remembered for as many as ten generations. There is no ultimate meaning for humans.[10]

This is a terribly depressing worldview, for, without a sense of meaning, human life is distressingly flat. In fact, the famed psychologist Viktor Frankl maintains that a person cannot be psychologically stable without a strong sense of meaning. Atheistic scientists don't seem to be bothered that their theories have eliminated meaning from humanity. The pursuit of knowledge gives scientists a very strong sense of meaning. Scientists dedicate their lives to solving (mostly minor) scientific problems and the sense of meaning they derive from this is supported by a society of other scientists who are studying similar questions. Scientists seem genuinely surprised to find that the general population do not have this option available to them. Without any sense of religion, most people are faced with a troublesome problem of constructing meaning in a society dominated by acquisition of wealth, possessions, and reputation. There is little mystery as to why, in the late 19th century, as materialism began to take hold in Western Society, Nietzsche said, 'God is dead.'

Now, at the opening of the 21st century, we find ourselves

living in a society produced from a science that is skeptical, if not totally hostile, to the concept of religion. This is a society whose economy is dependent on production and consumption of material goods, where we are bombarded from all sides with ads that assure us the purchase of this particular item will give happiness and meaning to our lives. In the face of all this, it is amazing that, a century after Nietzsche announced the death of God, 93% of the population in modern America still believe He exists. The fact that faith survives in such a barren environment is a profound indication that the meaning to life provided by religion is an innate human need that appears in some form in all human cultures. However, the presence of such intense religious conviction in our secular, materialistic society also clearly indicates a deep split in American society. This fissure leads to the tension between science and religion, a major aspect of which is the great evolution debate.

The Rise of Fundamentalism

The development of the materialistic worldview over the past two centuries has placed the traditional Christian, Muslim, and Jewish societies under tremendous pressure. All three religious groups recoil in horror from the empty nihilism that accompanies 'scientific' view of the world that is encompassed in the quotes given above. However, they have had difficulty in responding to it because science has obviously produced practical inventions and powerful logical techniques. By carefully observing and dissecting the material world, science has conquered many dreaded diseases, improved our ability to travel and communicate around the world, and has opened us to the understanding of processes that previously were completely mysterious. Thousands of years of religious practice had done none of this, which is one reason why organized religion, which was the dominant force in medieval society, lost so many battles to the forces of science.

One way to fight back at an enemy that has been so successful is to borrow from the enemy's tool bag. This is how some members of all three of the Western religions – Judaism, Christianity, and Islam – have responded to the threat of materialism. Because rationalism has worked so well in understanding the objective world, various sects have responded to Modernism by becoming increasingly rational themselves. Of course the new rationalism that arose within these religions was directed toward the interpretation of religious scripture, instead of toward the objective world. Rather than reading their religious texts (the Bible, Koran, or Torah) as symbols that pointed toward ineffable experiences, as was common in earlier times, some followers of the Abrahamic religions have begun to consider the texts as literal truth.[11] The sects that follow this approach are now termed Fundamentalist.

The Fundamentalists consider themselves to be at war with what they see as the immorality of Western secular society. The war is being fought on many fronts: cultural, political, and educational. Obviously, one of the places where this moral battle is being fought involves the biology curriculum of the public schools. As early as the 4th century, St. Augustine advised Christians to consider the history of the Earth as set forth in the Book of Genesis as myth, rather than taking it as literal truth. However, with the advent of Fundamentalism utter belief in the factual nature of the Scriptures has become an important tenet of faith among some people. With such a belief, the Fundamentalists have a moral imperative to continue the fight against what they view as the immoral forces of science. An example of this attitude is given by Alvin Plantinga in his essay against scientific theory of evolution:

> The first thing to see, as I said before, is that Christianity is indeed engaged in a conflict, a battle of unbelief. This contest or battle rages in many areas of contemporary culture – the

> courts, in the so-called media and the like – but perhaps most particularly in academia. And the second thing to see is that the important cultural forces such as science are not neutral with respect to this conflict ... we can't automatically take the word of the experts, because their word might be dead wrong from a Christian standpoint.[12]

With the Fundamentalists taking such a view there should be no surprise as to why they adopt such a strident tone in attacking Darwinism and the scientists who support it.

The Nature of the Debate

As tempting as it is to present the great evolution debate as a struggle between the materialistic view of science and the supernaturalism of Fundamentalists, we must realize that rather than being a black-and-white issue, the debate between religion and science involves a broad spectrum of viewpoints. On one side are the ultra-materialists such as Richard Dawkins and E.O. Wilson who use science to bolster a staunch atheism. The other extreme involves the 'Young-Earth' creationists who stolidly insist that the Earth is only a few thousand years old. Most of the advocates of Intelligent Design are less extreme than the Young-Earth creationists. They accept that a wide variety of different species may have populated the Earth during its long geologic history. However, they contend that all changes in species seen in the geologic record are the result of interventions by a Creator. Between these extremes lies a wide range of views. There are scientists and theologians who maintain that there is no conflict between their views of science and religion.[13] There are also scientists who, although materialists, accept the fact that religion has a role to play in society, as long as it doesn't overlap the domain of science.[14]

In this book I will concentrate much of my attention on the extreme views, because these absolutists set the tenor of the argument. However, before making my contribution to this complicated debate, I will use the next three chapters to define the terms I will be using. Without understanding clearly what I mean by terms such as 'science' and 'religion,' it is too easy to slide into a maze of emotional connotations that obscure the discussion.

Chapter 3
Two Ways of Knowing

Participants on both sides of the great evolution debate often present it as a dispute between science and religion in which there can be no compromise. E.O. Wilson has avowed this concept very succinctly in his book, *Consilience. The Unity of Knowledge,* which is an attempt to show how all knowledge can be unified under the guise of materialism.

> The uncomfortable truth is that the two beliefs (here Wilson is talking about the belief in science and the belief in religion) are not factually compatible. As a result those who hunger for both intellectual and religious truth will never acquire both in full measure.

Those who back science consider that they represent the modern, rational way of viewing the world. They trace their lineage to the struggles of Galileo and maintain that this worldview will eventually clear away the last vestiges of the dark superstitions that once shackled the human mind. The Fundamentalist Christians believe that the theory of evolution directly contradicts Biblical teachings and present themselves as trying to preserve a sense of morality against a cold system that utterly lacks any human values. With two groups starting from such different points of view is there any wonder that there is hardly any communication between them?

The major premise of this book will be that, rather than presenting antagonistic views of reality, science and religion are complementary ways of examining the world. Science studies the material world around us, whereas religion, through contemplative prayer or meditation, is the study of a transcendent reality that apparently lies beyond the material world of science. The conflict that many people describe between these two disciplines comes not from tenets that are inherent to either of them, but rather from attempts to express reality entirely within the confines of one or the other of these systems of thought. My view is similar to the concept of NOMA (Non-Overlapping Magisteria, where the word 'magisteria' refers to realms of expertise) put forth by Stephen J. Gould.[15] Gould also considers that science and religion occupy two distinct domains of expertise, but, as we will see in Chapter 5, there is a significant difference between NOMA and the ideas put forth in this book.

As a way to support this argument, let me note that conventionally there are two ways of knowing: objective and subjective knowledge. Objective knowledge is the knowledge of the world around us. It involves interaction between us and the material world that apparently exists 'out there'. Subjective knowledge is knowledge of the feelings that arise within us. Although Western society, particularly where dominated by materialism, seldom acknowledges this duality of knowledge (see that quote from Francis Crick in the previous chapter), we are continually immersed in it.

Ancient societies evolved two separate ways of describing these aspects of the world, which scholars, using Greek terms, call *logos*[16] and *mythos*. *Logos,* which is the root for the word 'logic', is the literal, rational way of talking about the objective world. *Mythos,* which is the root for the word 'myth', is a symbolic way of talking about the deeper aspects of the subjective world.

Because of the huge influence that science has on Western society, these days, when we talk about knowledge, we usually mean objective knowledge. This is the knowledge of science and math, of facts and figures. It is the knowledge that is described by the language of *logos*. Objective knowledge is more easily transmitted from one person to another than subjective knowledge because our language is closely tied to the material world. If we want to talk to a person about a tree we could point to the tree or even put our hands on it. Because our planet contains a variety of trees, our language has a huge number of terms to describe trees. When someone describes a tree as a pine, spruce, or a maple, we all know exactly what kind of tree to visualize. However, all objective facts have subjective connotations. Thus, like the blind men in the opening fable, just because we can 'lay our hands on' objective features, it doesn't mean that it is easy to use language to transmit knowledge about them or to reach a consensus as to what they mean.

In contrast to physical objects, language does a very poor job of describing subjective knowledge. When we are feeling unhappy, it is impossible for us to hook someone else up to our head so he or she could know exactly how unhappy we are. Thus, our words for subjective knowledge are slippery and have wide nuances of meaning. In fact, often we are feeling emotions that we cannot express at all. Subjective knowledge is the world of *mythos,* the world of poets, artists, and musicians who use various techniques to evoke emotions or knowledge that is beyond expression. Today, unfortunately, many people would say that the knowledge evoked by poetry, art, or music is hardly on par with the knowledge of science. Indeed, as noted in the last chapter, materialists would imply that, because our emotions are simply epiphenomena with little real importance, there is no great need to describe them in any detail.

These differences are reflected in the strong prejudicial contexts Western society appends to the words *objective* and *subjective.* The word 'objective' carries with it the connotation of being fair and true, whereas the word 'subjective' carries the sense of being biased and somewhat artificial. Indeed, often when one uses the word 'knowledge', one usually means only objective knowledge. Subjective knowledge, if it is considered at all, is usually considered to be something that exists only in your imagination.

To some extent, the structure of the human brain reflects this two-fold way of viewing the world. The brain consists of three major parts: the brain stem, the cerebellum and the cerebrum. The brain stem, located in the lowest and deepest area of the brain, controls the body functions that are critical to life, such as respiration and heartbeat. The cerebellum lies on the back and rear of the brain and is in charge of coordinating fine body movements. The cerebrum, which is largest portion of the brain, controls most of our cognitive functions. It is divided into two hemispheres by a deep fissure that runs along the length of the brain from front to back. A narrow stem of nerves called the corpus callosum join the two hemispheres.

Each hemisphere of the cerebrum controls the motion and senses of the opposite side of the body. The nerves from the right side of the body go to the left hemisphere and those from the left side of the body go to the right side of the brain. In addition, each hemisphere has a different way of processing thoughts. The left brain takes a linear, logical, verbal, analytic approach to solving problems. In contrast, the right brain takes a nonverbal, intuitive, spatial approach that is based upon holistic perception of overall patterns. Although the details of how the brain works is complex, it is no great stretch to suggest that the left brain controls *logos*, our logical view of objective reality, whereas the right brain is the seat of *mythos*.

When modern society downplays the importance of subjective knowledge it ignores the fact that for most of us it is the subjective world that provides the biggest problems and the greatest joys in our lives. As an example, consider the following situation:

> *You meet a particularly attractive person of the opposite sex at a party. He or she is impeccably attired, has an alluring smile, and laughing blue eyes that sparkle as he or she looks as you. This is a person you would like to get to know better. You smile back and begin a conversation…*

Here is your problem: You know the outer appearance of this person and you know your inner response to this appearance. However, you really don't know how you appear to him or her. Sure, you know what you are wearing and what you look like in the mirror, but you really cannot be certain whether the way you act carries with it an aura of confidence or whether it presents a subtle sense of artifice. Neither do you know whether the person you have met is as smitten with you as you are with him or her or whether he or she is just being polite. In other words, whereas you are aware of your subjective response to this person's objective appearance, you are also painfully aware that you have no idea at all of how that person is responding to you.

Thus, although our culture may consider subjective knowledge as being less important than objective knowledge, in our everyday lives we are continually struggling with the tension between the 'outside' world and our subjective response to it. Most of the problems we have in our relationships arise from this clash. Largely because of the difficulty in verbalizing feelings and emotions, partners often find it difficult to communicate to each other. One of the great ironies, therefore, of Western society, is that, although we are all troubled by subjective feelings, according to the materialist worldview, these feelings are not very important. They are regarded as products of chemical or electrical reactions within our brains.

In this book I maintain that science is a manifestation of objective knowledge (i.e. of *logos*), whereas religion is a manifestation of subjective knowledge (i.e. of *mythos*). It is easy to understand how science arises from objective knowledge. Science involves knowledge that is based upon observation and measurement, and clearly one can observe and measure only material objects (or the energy produced by movement of these objects). It is much more difficult to see how religion can be related to subjective knowledge because many modern religions try to present their tenets as solid material truth (i.e. as *logos* instead of *mythos*). Furthermore, these days it is common to dismiss the beliefs of others as being 'only myth', suggesting that myth, and *mythos,* are not important in our modern scheme of things. It is critical to note, however, that the experiences upon which religion is based are internal and highly subjective. The religious experience is not merely a sensory experience; it also involves a change in perception. In other words, just as you cannot tell what another person *really* thinks about you, you cannot tell whether or not the person next to you is having a religious experience.

For example, perhaps you are on a long meditation retreat and in a moment of boredom you cast a glance at the woman who is sitting beside you. She is meditating with perfect posture and looks intensely absorbed. Is she having a deep spiritual experience or is she merely thinking about what she's going to do when this boring meditation session is over? You simply cannot tell. Similarly, the people who were on the road to Damascus with Saul of Tarsus on the day that Saul underwent his historic conversion did not experience the same rapture that Saul did.

Religion is, therefore, an intensely subjective experience and differs in almost every way from the objective world of science. Before we can understand the bitter debate over evolution and creationism, we have to understand the roots of these two kinds of knowledge. That is what we will investigate in the next two chapters.

Chapter 4
The World of Science

Science is the process by which modern humans understand the phenomena of the natural world around us. Rather than philosophizing about the material world, science involves observing, counting, and measuring aspects of the physical world and using the results to establish theories of how those features came to be. The process by which these theories have been developed is known as the scientific method. The scientific method evolved in the seventeenth century and since then humanity's understanding of the physical world has grown phenomenally. The richness of our modern economy, our ability to travel quickly to anywhere in the globe (and even into outer space), and our ability to communicate instantly with people in any place on Earth is a tangible result of the progress that the scientific way of thinking has brought humanity.

One of the key aspects of science is reductionism, which involves studying the physical world by breaking it down into its constituent parts. The world around us is forbiddingly complex. To understand it, scientists concentrate on studying one small aspect of it at a time. For example, thunderstorms are violent phenomena that surely induced awe in pre-scientific humans. To determine how a thunderstorm operates, science breaks the phenomenon down to the following questions:

How does moisture circulate through the atmosphere?
How do convection cells operate to dissipate heat?
How much heat is given off when water vapor condenses into droplets?
How does static electricity form?

The answers to each of these questions alone may not directly tell us how thunderstorms form. However, using them together, one can develop a reasonable explanation for the origin of thunderstorms. More importantly, the answers to each of these questions can be applied to understanding many other phenomena. This example points to one of the great strengths of reductionism. The insights obtained from studying a small aspect of one problem can be used to help explain other problems, many of which may be only distantly related to the original question.

The Scientific Method

Traditionally, the scientific method consists of four steps. The first involves **observation of facts.** These are observations or measurements that any reasonable person will make from the data available. Next comes the **formation of a hypothesis or hypotheses** that are designed to explain the data. In the ideal scientific process one would postulate more than one hypothesis. In the next step, one **designs experiments to test the hypotheses.** If you were dealing with a science such as physics and chemistry you might design experiments that you could conduct in a lab. If you were studying a historical science, such as geology, ecology, or astronomy, you use your hypothesis to predict relations you would find in the natural world. You then test the hypothesis by looking for the relations that it predicts. If your experiments are well designed, you should be able to discount all but one of the hypotheses. This will allow the scientist to **establish a theory that explains the observations.**

Although this may sound terribly erudite to some, most of us use the scientific method in everyday life. Suppose your teenage son has just come into the house with the news that his car won't start. What could be wrong? An automobile is a highly complex instrument and there are many things that could keep it from running. However, since it was running when your son came home last night, you can reduce the problem to a few possibilities:

perhaps the battery is dead, maybe the battery's not dead but there is a bad connection to the battery terminals, or perhaps the starter engine is dead. Armed with these possibilities you go out to your son's car and try to start it yourself. You find that the starter doesn't even turn over, even after you clean the battery terminals. However, the car does start when you connect jumper cables from the battery of your car to the battery in your son's car. Clearly the battery in your son's car is dead. Now, of course you need to make an investigation (and maybe some more experiments) to determine if the battery had simply discharged (maybe your son left the headlights on last night or maybe there is a short somewhere in the car's circuits) or whether the car needs a new battery.

In solving this simple problem you have used the scientific method. First you were presented with a series of facts; in this instance it was simply that the car didn't start. Then you developed hypotheses; here you had three: the cause was either the battery, the connection between the battery and the starter, or the starter. Then you performed a series of experiments that allowed you to eliminate the hypotheses that didn't work.

Before I go much further, I must discuss the word 'theory'. Proponents of Intelligent Design argue that evolution is 'only a theory'. By this, they imply that one can substitute any other theory for it, such as the theory of Intelligent Design. This confusion comes about because the word 'theory' has two distinctly different connotations. These are, as given by the Oxford English Dictionary:

1. It is a scheme or system of ideas or statements held as an explanation or account of a group of facts or phenomena; a hypothesis that has been confirmed or established by observation or experiment, and in propounded or accepted as accounting for the known facts; a statement of what are held to be general laws, principles, or causes of something known or observed.

2. It is a hypothesis proposed as an explanation; hence a mere hypothesis, speculation, conjecture; an idea or set of ideas about something; an individual view of notion.

The problem arises because, when scientists talk about the theory of evolution, at least with respect the manner by which life has changed over Earth's history, they are using the first definition. Evolution is a profoundly well-tested theory that has stood up to 150 years of intense scientific tests. However, though they may not realize it, when scientists talk about how the theory of evolution impacts our view of reality, such as comments that evolution is mechanical, random, and purposeless, they are using the second definition of the word. This, of course, is the connotation that the advocates of Intelligent Design think of when they say, 'evolution is only a theory'.

Unfortunately, there is no easy way to solve this contextual confusion because no adequate synonym for 'theory' exists that applies only to one of the definitions above. As a result, I must use both connotations in this book. When I talk about a theory with purely a scientific connotation I will use the first definition, but when I talk about the social impacts of a theory I will use the second definition.

There are three important points about the scientific method that makes it so powerful:

1) A theory is not scientific unless it can be tested. This means that nothing is sacred in science, not even concepts that have been accepted for a long time. Every concept is subject to testing and every theory is susceptible to revision. The philosopher Karl Popper called this property *falsifiability*. A scientific theory is testable if it can be disproved or falsified. If it cannot be falsified, it is not a scientific theory.

2) To be valid, an experiment must be reproducible. This means that other scientists must be able to verify your results by doing your experiments themselves. The results of your research will be suspect unless others can reproduce them.

3) Although a set of experiments may disprove a theory, they can never PROVE one. In other words, there is always some sense of doubt about the theories of science, and experiments designed to test one set of hypotheses can also be used to test all the observations upon which those hypotheses are based. This is the primary reason why Creation Science is not science. Rather than establishing theories and trying to *disprove* them, Creationists cobble together bits and pieces of data from the geologic and biologic literature and use them to *'prove'* statements like 'The Earth is 6,000 years old'.

Because of these three points, the growth of scientific knowledge has been dynamic; each theory set forth to explain one problem introduces further questions to be answered. This, of course, is why science has progressed so rapidly. The progress of science, however, is seldom linear. From time to time new theories arise that completely overturn the established concepts. When this happens, science suddenly finds a whole new way of looking at the physical world. These changes are known as scientific revolutions or paradigm shifts. Paradigm shifts occur in science on all levels, from minor discoveries that appear on a regular basis to infrequent revolutions (such as that instituted by Darwin's theory of evolution), which reverberate through the whole society.

Scientific Paradigms

Because science deals exclusively with objective knowledge, many scientists contend that the process of scientific investigation is entirely an objective process. However, if science were free of subjectivity, then all scientists looking at a set of data would come to the same conclusion. Such consensus hardly ever happens. Any scientist will tell you that the world of science is rife with controversies that are as divisive and fiercely fought as the debate among the blind men about the nature of the elephant. The problem is, however, that the scientists involved in these controversies are all basing their arguments on the same data. The controversies are produced entirely by the subjective interpretation of this data.

Because of this inherent subjectivity, science operates within a milieu of convention, premises, and assumptions that govern the kinds of experiments that are conducted. Thomas Kuhn called this milieu a *paradigm* and maintained that the development of all fields of science follows a similar pattern.[17] In pre-modern science each investigator had to formulate his (most early scientists were men) own view of how the system he is studying operates. Eventually a major scientist came along who took all the earlier work and combined it into a unifying paradigm that would control the questions and experiments that later workers used. After a while, however, clues appeared suggesting that the paradigm didn't perfectly describe nature. At first scientists ignored these clues because, despite the flaws, the current theory still did a pretty good job describing the data. However, as more and more data built up that didn't fit the theory, a scientist appeared who looked at the assembled facts in a different way. This lead to a new theory, and a scientific revolution, or paradigm shift, occurred. The new paradigm incorporated several aspects of nature that the previous paradigm had ignored and usually lead to a whole new set of questions that could not have been asked under the old paradigm.

The science of optics is a good example of this process. Previous to Newton, there was no unifying theory of how light behaved, so that each investigator had to construct a theory from the ground up. This period is shown in Figure 1 as the four light lines.

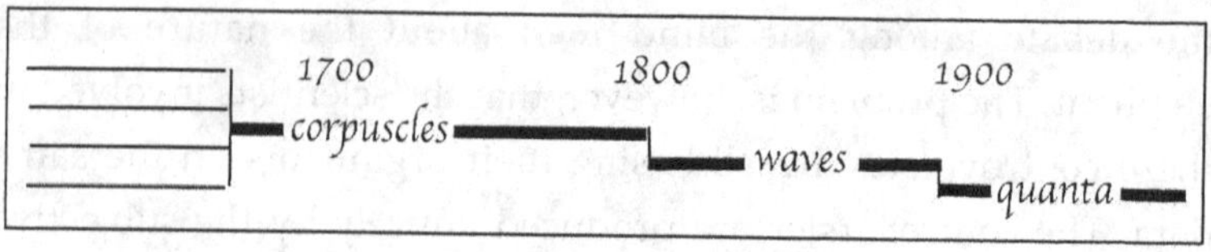

Figure 1 Time line showing the changes in paradigms for the science of optics.

In the later years of the seventeenth century, Newton published *Optiks,* which provided scientists working on light a theory or paradigm that they could test with further research. Newton considered light to be made up of tiny particles or corpuscles. This concept was superseded in the early years of the nineteenth century by the theory that light occurred as waves moving through a medium. This paradigm, in turn, was supplanted around the turn of the twentieth century by the concept that light (along with radio waves and X-rays) was simply energy, or electromagnetic radiation, that was emitted in fixed wavelengths (or quanta) from a substance that had been heated to a high enough temperature. These quanta may manifest as either waves of particles.

Kuhn argued that, because a paradigm controls (both consciously and unconsciously) how scientists view their discipline, it also determines the nature of the experiments that scientists conduct. Scientific paradigms are so powerful because they cause scientists to focus experiments on testing or enlarging these aspects of the natural world to which the paradigm may be applied. However, this strength is also a weakness, because it is impossible for a scientist to think of experiments that lie outside of the paradigm. For example, in the nineteenth century, physicists spent a lot of time designing experiments to measure the presence of *ether,* the substance that they thought filled interstellar space. Experiments of this kind seemed reasonable at that time because the prevalent view held that without ether there would be no way for light waves to move through space. However, those experiments abruptly ceased once scientists recognized that light was electromagnetic radiation. Because electromagnetic radiation could move through a vacuum, once the electromagnetic theory was accepted; it was no longer necessary to postulate the existence of interstellar ether.

Those paradigm shifts that involve purely scientific outlooks usually take place on time scales on the order of a decade, but two scientific revolutions that strongly contradicted the teachings of the Christian Church took more than a century to complete. The first was the transition from geocentrism, the concept that the Earth was the center of the solar system (in fact the center of the universe), to heliocentrism, which involved the realization that the Earth actually revolved around the sun. As we noted in Chapter 2, Copernicus' theory that the Earth revolved around the sun was published in 1543, the year the great astronomer died. The heliocentric theory languished until Galileo published his book, *Starry Messenger,* in 1610. There then followed a long period of controversy that was not finally settled until late in the seventeenth century with the publication Newton's book, *Principia Mathematica,* which showed how gravity affects the orbits of planets (Figure 2).

Figure 2 Time line for the Copernican revolution, which involved the transition from the view that the Earth was the center of the solar system to the recognition that the sun is the center. 1543 = publication of Copernicus' theory, 1610 = publication of Galileo's support for the theory, 1687 = publication of Newton's *Principia Mathematica,* 1992 = Catholic Church finally admits that Galileo was right.

The paradigm shift for evolution took place on a similar time scale (Figure 3). Benoit de Maillet first put forth the concept of evolution in 1735, but it languished in the shadows for more than 100 years before the publication of *The Origin of the Species.*

Within 10 years of the publication of Darwin's book most biologists accepted his theory, although, as noted above, public disbelief in the theory persists to the present day.

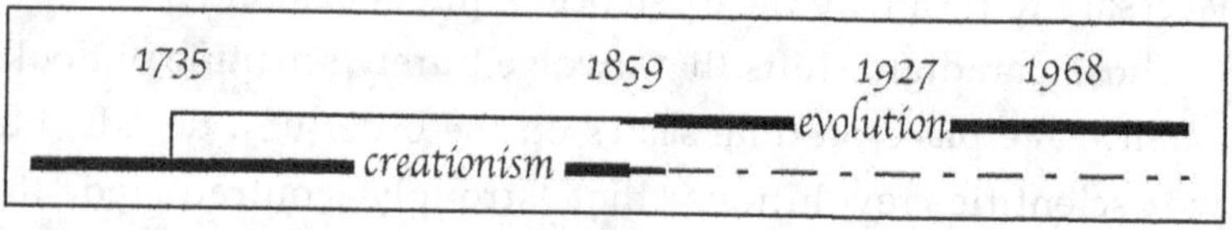

Figure 3 Time line for the Darwinian revolution. 1735 = first espousal for the theory, 1859 = publication of *Origin of the Species*, 1927 = Scopes trial, 1968 = US Supreme Court turned down laws banning the teaching of evolution.

The examples above clearly demonstrate that the operation of science is not as cold and rational as some scientists would like us to believe. Not only do scientific discoveries change the way we view the world; the views we hold toward the world determine the kind of scientific discoveries that can be made. Just as it is inconceivable that physicists today would conduct experiments to determine the nature of ether in interstellar space, it is equally inconceivable that either heliocentric astronomy or Darwinian evolution could have been discovered before the Renaissance and the Reformation weakened the Catholic dogma that controlled the view Western society had of the world.[18]

Science and Metaphysics

If you were to ask most scientists about the relation between science and metaphysics they may wonder what you are talking about. Physics is a field of science but metaphysics, the study of the ultimate nature of reality, is a field of philosophy. As I mentioned at the beginning of the chapter, the role of science in our society is to study the material world, not to philosophize about it. Thus, many scientists would say that metaphysics should have nothing to do with science. By saying so, however, they ignore the fact that scientific investigation was impossible until some portions of society began to develop a naturalistic view of the world. The contention that all phenomena in the natural world have a natural cause, which is inherent in naturalism, is clearly a metaphysical concept. It postulates that there is a natural world 'out there' and that things happening in this world can be understood by observation and reason.

The metaphysical implication of naturalism is a hidden premise upon which all science is constructed. It is 'hidden' because it is so pervasive that most scientists don't even consider that there may be other ways of viewing reality. Because few scientists are aware of the metaphysical implications of their profession, it is easy for many of them to slide from naturalism to materialism. It is very reasonable for scientists to contend that 'phenomena in the physical world have natural causes' because, by holding this assumption, science has made incredible advances over the past three hundred years. However, it is not valid to maintain that science *proves* that 'the physical world is all there is', because, as noted in the previous chapter, science can only speak authoritatively about the objective world; it cannot make any valid comment about the existence or non-existence of a transcendental reality. The scientific absolutists, such as E.O. Wilson, who maintain that materialistic science can explain the religious experience, are either blissfully unaware of the limitations of science or they choose to ignore that these limitations exist. In many ways they are similar to the Creationists who maintain that scientific view of evolution is wrong because it doesn't agree with the ancient legends recorded in the Book of Genesis. Both are like the blind men who try to interpret the nature of the elephant by examining its trunk.

Science and Creativity

When one mentions the term 'creativity' most people think of works of art, rather than science. However, creativity is just as critical to science as it is to art, literature, or music. The best scientist is not the person who makes the most measurements or the one who makes the best measurements. Rather, he or she is a person who can make the conceptual jump that explains trends no one had previously recognized. Leon Borgman, who was a member of the National Academy of Engineers, and obviously a highly accomplished researcher, made the point that in many ways the scientific method described at the beginning of this chapter is a lie.[19] He pointed out that real research is a messy process that involves chasing a lot of dead ends and fumbling in the dark with a mass of data before a scientist discovers how these data are related. The logical construction outlined by the scientific method is a framework that is laid upon your research AFTER the answer has been determined. In other words, although science and mathematics are usually expressed as involving a left-brain process that is entirely logical, the true operation of science also involves the right-brain processes of intuition and creativity, operations that relate to subjective knowledge.

Perhaps one of the best examples of the use of intuition in science is the discovery of the structure of benzene in 1865 by Fredrich Kekulé. To give you some idea of the problem Kekulé was dealing with, we need to understand the situation of chemistry in the 1850s and 1860s. Much of what we consider to be basic to chemistry today – valance, chemical bonding, thermodynamics, and the structure of chemical compounds – was still unknown. Chemists were struggling in the dark, trying to put together theories that would help explain the complexities of the chemical compounds they were encountering. They could determine the composition of many compounds, but how the atoms were put together to make those compounds was still a mystery.

One of the groups of compounds that chemists recognized at that time was the alkanes or methane series. The simplest organic compound in this series is methane (CH_4), which consists of one atom of carbon that is bounded to four hydrogens (Figure 4).

When two methane molecules are combined so that the two carbon atoms are bounded to each other, this produces the compound ethane (C_2H_6). Similarly, adding another carbon to the ethane chain produces propane (C_3H_8). It is clear from these examples that organic compounds consisting of simple carbon chains bonded to hydrogen contain far more hydrogen than carbon. Thus, a compound with six carbon atoms (hexane) should contain 14 hydrogens (Figure 4).

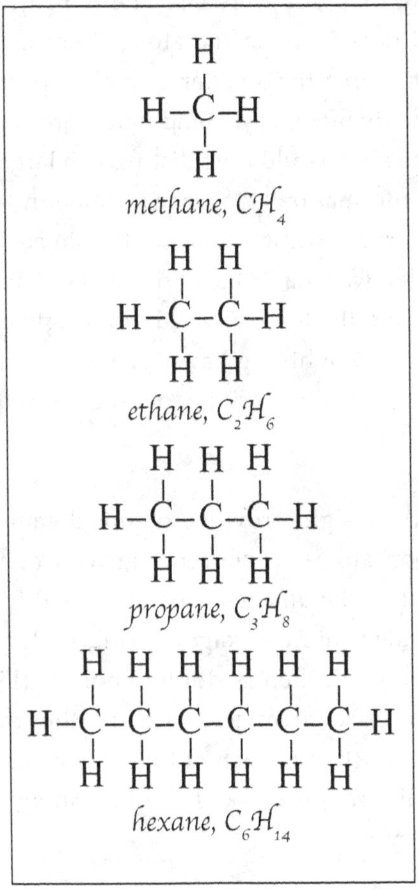

Figure 4 Structure of the alkanes, or simple chain series of carbohydrate molecules.

Benzene (C_6H_6) was one compound that did not behave in this way at all. Like hexane, benzene contains six carbon atoms, but unlike hexane it has only six hydrogens. What was going on in this compound so that it had so many fewer hydrogens than does hexane? This is the problem that Kekulé was struggling with when:

> I was sitting, writing at my text books; but the work did not progress; my thoughts were elsewhere. I turned my chair to the fire and dozed. Again the atoms were gamboling before my eyes. This time the smaller groups kept modestly in the background. My mental eye, tendered more acute by repeated visions of the kind, could now distinguish larger structures, of manifold conformation: long rows, sometimes more closely fitted together; all twining and twisting in snake-like motion. But look! What was that? One of the snakes had seized hold of its own tail, and the form whirled mockingly before my eyes. As if by a flash of lightning I awoke; and this time also I spent the rest of the night working on the consequences of the hypothesis.[20]

Working from the insight provided by this dream, Kekulé postulated that carbon atoms in benzene, instead of forming single chains as it does in the alkanes, were arranged in rings. The six carbons are bonded into a hexagonal ring with three of the six bonds between them being double bonds (Figure 5). The hydrogen atoms are arranged outside the ring, with one hydrogen atom attached to each of the carbon atoms. This major conceptual breakthrough marked the beginning of the field of organic chemistry.

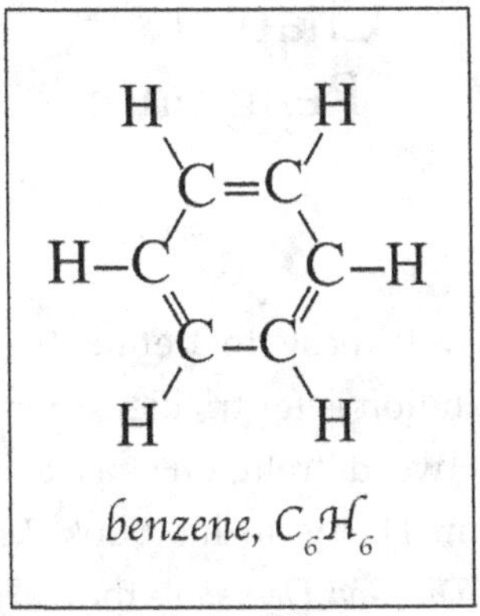

Figure 5 The structure of benzene as developed by Frederich Kekulé from his dream.

Very few scientists are as open about their dream life as was Kekulé, but there is little doubt that the jump from observation to theory involves an intuition that is not very different from the creativity employed by poets and artists. It is ironic, therefore, that the very progress of science depends on those aspects of reality that are invisible and ineffable, aspects that materialists would maintain are only by-products of chemical reactions in our brains. In other words, the progress of science, our objective study of the phenomenal world, comes from the subjective portion of reality that materialists maintain is not important.

Chapter 5
Religion

Although it is relatively easy to define the scope of Science, getting a grasp on Religion is far trickier. To many intellectuals in Western Society, the word 'religion' has a decidedly negative connotation. Like Sam Harris in his book *The End of Faith* and Richard Dawkins in *The God Delusion,* they argue that religion is a throwback to ancient superstitions and that mankind would be better off if we learned to live without it.[21] This view is not surprising considering that the growth of modern secular democratic society has involved a 400-year long struggle against the restraints of the religious establishment. To many, the battle between Evolutionists and Creationists (or the advocates of Intelligent Design) is seen as the last remnants of the struggle that goes back to the persecution of Galileo. In addition, religion today hardly seems to be a positive force in the world. Almost daily we read news reports describing horrible acts of violence and intolerance that are committed in the name of religion. Considering the mayhem that has been perpetrated (and unfortunately continues to be perpetrated) on humanity by people who maintain that they are acting for a religious purpose, maybe the materialists are right. Isn't religion an old habit that has little value to modern life which we'd be better off getting rid of?

If you believe that only objective knowledge matters, as Dawkins maintains in *The God Delusion,* then the answer to the question posed above is 'yes.' Objective knowledge, however, is concerned only with things we can touch or measure. It has nothing to say about values. Religion is important because it is based on subjective knowledge, and it is our subjective view of the world that establishes the basis of our values and governs how we relate to others. More importantly, religion is one of the prime ways that humans derive meaning to their lives. Many of us would say that the indifferent universe described in the quote by Richard Dawkins in Chapter 2 is simply wrong. Most of us have an inherent feeling that the universe makes sense, though seldom are we able to provide objective reasons why this is so.

If religion is so important to society then why does it get such bad press? As we noted in Chapter 2, one of the impacts of the scientific revolution has been the rise of Fundamentalism in the Abrahamic religions. By reading the symbolism of religion as literal fact, Fundamentalists erect impenetrable walls between each of the World's religions. Not only that, because Fundamentalists believe that they are struggling to save humanity from the horrors of a cold, Godless, secular society, many of them have assumed militant, intolerant, and sometime violent tactics to attain their goals. The moralistic and often arrogant views that Fundamentalists espouse about modern social issues are abhorrent to most tolerant people in our society and clearly reflect poorly on the whole field of religion.

The Commonality of Religions

If we can look through the fog of *logos*, we would see that, as mystics of all traditions have maintained for centuries, the World's religions spring from a common mystical experience. Aldous Huxley called this commonality the *perennial philosophy*[22] and, though the term has not been used much, Huxley's views have been stressed in many of recent books on religion.[23] If all religions arise from a common root, why is it that religious wars have cursed humanity throughout history? The tension between religions arises because the mystical experience, the basis of all religion, is ineffable. To express it, all religions rely upon symbols. When a person practices a religion, the symbols of that religion become imprinted in their mind. When she or he undergoes a spiritual experience, it is invariably expressed through those symbols. Unfortunately, the symbols used by various religions are different and often mutually contradictory. Only by reading the symbols as *mythos* rather than *logos,* do we see the commonality of religions.

One of the best expressions of the common basis of the World's Religions comes from participants of the Snowmass Conference. The Snowmass Conference was a meeting of spiritual teachers from the Buddhist, Hindu, Islamic, Jewish, Native American, Russian Orthodox, Protestant, and Roman Catholic faiths who gathered regularly at the St. Benedict's Monastery in Snowmass, Colorado in the 1980s.[24] As a result of the conference, they produced a list of the features common to all religions. Four of the most important features are:

1. The world religions bear witness to the experience of Ultimate Reality to which they give various names: Brahman, Allah, (the) Absolute, God and the Great Spirit. The key word in this sentence is 'experience'. The world's religions are not elaborate fairy tales about how the world came to be, as most atheists would maintain. Rather, religions are based upon what is called the mystical experience, an experience that conveys a sense of unity with nature, an infusion of love for the beings within it, and a feeling of certainty that there is a deep meaning to life.

The fact that all religions stem from a similar experience doesn't mean that all religions are the same. Obviously they are not. Each religion has its own view of the mystical experience and its own rituals for accessing it. However, the common source does explain why the mystical writings of all religions are so similar. Because Ultimate Reality is ineffable, many mystics try to communicate using parables. The parables of Jesus, the Sufis, Hassidic Jews, and of Zen Buddhism are far more similar to each other than to the dogmas of the religions to which they nominally belong.

2. Ultimate Reality cannot be limited by any name or concept. Because Ultimate Reality lies beyond words, we cannot describe it with words; we can only hint at it with symbols. To understand this, imagine what it would be like if you grew up blind in a world where everyone else is also blind. You can hear the sounds of flowing water or wind in the trees, feel the sun or rain on your face, and smell the sweetness of flowers or the earthiness of the soil, but the main way you negotiate your way through your environment will be by touch. Even though you may be able to get along very well in the world, there will be many things that you will not be aware of simply because you cannot experience them without being able to see.

What would happen if one day you are suddenly granted the gift of sight? How would you tell your friends about the puffy white clouds that are floating in the blue sky above their heads? Not only would your friends have no idea of what clouds are, they wouldn't even know what you mean by the words white or blue. Color would be a totally alien concept to them. Just like the blind men in our parable cannot conceive of the whole elephant based upon their limited experience, your friends cannot understand any object or concept that can only be sensed by vision alone. Of course, if you were the first person ever to see, you wouldn't even have words such as 'cloud' or 'blue' with which to describe your experience. The same is true for those who experience Ultimate Reality. The experience is real enough, but there simply is no way they can describe it to others.

The fact that Ultimate Reality lies beyond all concepts explains the amazing variety of religions in the world. How each person experiences Ultimate Reality depends strongly on the cultural background of that person. A Muslim praying to Allah is unlikely to have visions of the Shiva, nor is a Catholic likely to have visions of Muhammad. The protean nature of the religious experience is well demonstrated by the life of Ramakrishna, the Indian sage who lived from 1836 to 1886. Ramakrishna was a devotee of the Hindu goddess Kali and commonly was enveloped in rapture while praying to her. During one period in his life, Ramakrishna took up Islamic practice. He removed all Hindu images from his room, chanted verses of the Koran in Arabic, and preformed the cycles of prostrations praising Allah that Muslims do every day. After a short time he was graced with a vision of Muhammad who merged with his being and lifted his awareness to a mystic union with Allah. Another time while gazing on a painting of the Virgin Mary, a sense of Christ's nature came forth from the icon and penetrated into the heart of his consciousness. So taken was he by this that he couldn't enter the temple to Kali for three days.[25]

These stories demonstrate the importance of realizing the value of *mythos* in our lives. The *mythos* in each religion is pointing to an experience you cannot understand until you experience it yourself. This also means that no religion has the sole answer to the nature of Ultimate Reality. Because religions are trying to hint at experiences that are beyond description, it is inherently impossible to describe the experience completely. Each religion has a special way to approach this problem, but this doesn't invalidate the approach of other religions.

A good example of the variety of religious expression is the way the world's religions envision Ultimate Reality. When most members of Western society think of religion they think of a personal God. It is difficult for most Westerners to understand that a number of religions, Buddhism and Taoism foremost among them, are non-theistic. In non-theistic religions, Ultimate Reality has no personality. The theistic religions (Judaism, Christianity, and Islam for example), which worship a transcendent loving creator, appear to be an entirely different species from the non-theistic religions. It seems impossible for these two types of religions to have any common root. However, these contrasting views of Ultimate Reality coexist quite easily in Hinduism, one of the world's oldest religions. Depending on one's proclivities, a good Hindu may worship Nirguna Brahman (God without attributes) or Saguna Brahman (God with attributes). Huston Smith uses the following analogy to compare theistic and non-theistic approaches to the Ultimate Reality:

> If one is struggling against a current it is comforting to have a master swimmer by one's side. It is equally important that there be a shore, solid and serene, that lies beyond the struggle as the terminus of one's splashings.[26]

Ken Wilber in his book *Integral Spirituality* maintains that this paradox arises because Ultimate Reality manifests in first, second and third person. The first person manifestation is the feeling a person has when having a religious experience. The second person manifestation is the sense of a loving God that is inherent in the theistic religion. The third person manifestation is sense of Godhead, the ultimate from which all reality arises, which is described by the non-theistic religions.

3. Ultimate Reality is the ground of infinite potentiality and actualization. This means that much of our creativity and insight comes from the Ultimate Reality, and not, as the materialists would maintain, simply from chemical reactions in our brain. Thus, as you open yourself to the Ultimate Reality, you will gain access to greater creativity and insight.

4. Faith is opening, accepting, and responding to Ultimate Reality. Faith in this sense precedes every belief system. Although in the English language we usually consider the words *faith* and *belief* to be synonyms, there is an important difference between them. In many ways 'belief' is the opposite of 'faith'. As Anthony DeMello, the Jesuit mystic, says, 'Beliefs give you a lot of security, but faith is insecurity'.[27] *Faith* produces insecurity because it opens you to something that is unknown and indescribable. It involves being open to the inexpressible experiences that arise when one begins to get in touch with Ultimate Reality. In contrast, *belief* involves ossifying these inexpressible experiences into solid symbols.

When one turns *faith* into *belief* one is in danger of turning *mythos* into *logos*, and when that happens, suddenly the vast commonality that unites all religions disappears and differences appear that many people will be ready to die for. Unfortunately these differences appear only as perceptions. As the old Zen saying goes, 'When the wise man points to the moon, all the fool sees is the finger'. Most of the debate over which religion is the TRUE religion is a debate over the qualities inherent in the finger; it has very little to do with the moon. When the Creationists say that, because evolution contradicts a literal interpretation of the Bible, evolution is incompatible with religion, they are talking about the finger, not the moon. Likewise, when the neo-atheists write passionately about how religion is a curse on humanity, they too are talking only about the finger; they are utterly unaware that the moon exists.

The conflict between *mythos* and *logos* is also at the heart of the struggle between the priests and the prophets that has troubled Abrahamic religions throughout their history. The job of the priests is to protect the teachings of the religion; the priests may know the words very well, but they may not have experienced the mystical truth behind them. Naturally, they become indignant when someone comes along whose teaching is derived directly from personal experience and apparently contradicts religious dogma. This is the reason why the Jewish priests in Jerusalem gladly let Pontius Pilate crucify Jesus and why in the 13th century the Catholic Church excommunicated Meister Eckhart. This also explains why, in the Middle Ages, the mystical Sufis continually ran afoul of the Islamic clerics.

The conflict between *logos* and *mythos* is also the reason why so many people today would say that they are spiritual but not religious. These people recognize that there is a spiritual side to existence. However, they maintain that religions, which in modern times have increasingly interpreted their teachings in terms of *logos*, seem to be more interested in spreading a dogma than opening people to spiritual values. To go back to the Zen parable, to many people, modern religions seem more interested in closely analyzing the finger rather than helping one experience the moon.

The Mystical Experience

As we noted above, the mystic traditions maintain that we are immersed within an Ultimate Reality. Most of the time, we are not aware of this reality in which we swim because our ego separates it into subjective and objective aspects (Figure 6). With our attention diverted by the constant chatter of thoughts that arise from our ego, we are hardly aware of the Ultimate Reality that surrounds us. We go through life continually talking to ourselves, judging others, telling ourselves grand stories about us as heroes, planning great deeds, obsessing about the past, or worrying about the future. From time to time, glimpses of Ultimate Reality may appear in the form of inspiration, intuition, or creativity. Most of us, however, would attribute these insights to something operating within our own head without recognizing their ultimate source. Mystics tell us that, if we could simply stop the mental chatter that occupies us most of the time, the wonder of Ultimate Reality would shine through. As the great Sufi poet Rumi says:

> If you could get rid of yourself just once,
> The secret of secrets would become open to you
> The face of the unknown, hidden behind the universe
> Would appear in the mirror of your perception.

In his book, *New Seeds of Contemplation,* the Catholic monk Thomas Merton echoes with similar words:

> One of the greatest paradoxes of the mystical life is this: that a man cannot enter into the deepest center of himself and pass

through that center into God, unless he can pass entirely out of himself and empty himself.[28]

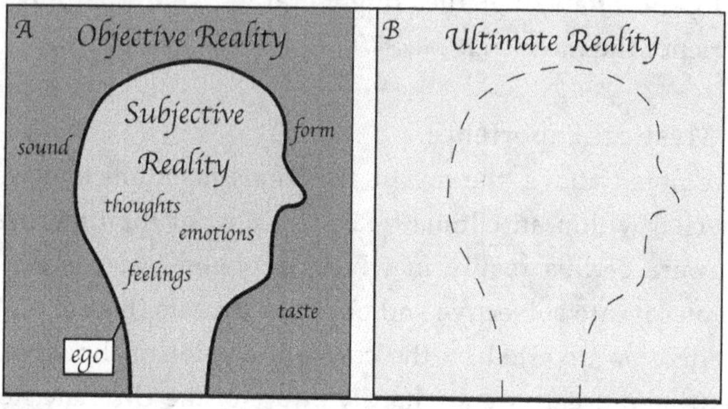

Figure 6 Diagram showing: A. how the formation of our ego separates the world into an objective and subjective reality and B. how Ultimate Reality appears when the ego dissolves.

The goal of all mystical traditions is to erode away that heavy sense of ego that we all carry around with us. This can be done in many ways. In the Buddhist tradition one uses meditation to observe the operation of ego. The more one watches how ego forms, the less solid it becomes. Christians and Jews use contemplative prayer to put themselves in touch with the Ultimate Reality that lies beyond it all. Sufis use ecstatic dance to make the connection. Regardless of the technique used, if you keep the practice up long enough, the power of the ego slowly begins to dissolve and you become more and more attuned to insights from Ultimate Reality. As this happens, you naturally become less interested in pursuing your own agenda and more concerned about the welfare of others. Eventually a shattering experience arises when you finally break through the boundaries of ego and realize that you are inseparable from Ultimate Reality. This experience is called enlightenment. Although it was originally a term applied to experiences in Eastern religions, these days it is commonly applied to the deep realization common to all religions.[29]

When the walls of the ego crumble, allowing us to see the Ultimate Reality that surrounds us, another interesting thing happens; the distinction between self and other disappears (Figure 6B). With this, the division we made between objective and subjective knowledge evaporates. Mystics say that when one experiences the Ultimate Reality, one gains an insight that can accommodate both objective and subjective knowledge. Herein lies the critical flaw in Gould's NOMA theory, which maintains that science and religion are fields that shouldn't overlap. Certainly, the way we normally look at reality (Figure 6A), it appears as if objective and subjective realities are separate. With this view, it is reasonable to maintain that science and religion are mutually exclusive endeavors. However, when we realize that both of them are only aspects of a single Ultimate Reality, then the fields of Science and Religion must overlap. This concept is inherent in Ken Wilber's book, *The Marriage of Sense and Soul: Integrating Science and Religion*. Wilber points out that science and religion can be unified if science acknowledges that there is more to reality than the material world and if religion recognizes that the spiritual life is based upon experience, not adherence to any dogma.

If we really want to understand the world around us, each of us must be able to integrate objective and subjective reality into the mystical whole. Unfortunately, most of us have not reached that state of insight and, to us, the world appears as if we are separate from our surroundings. For this reason, in this book I treat the world as if it consists of an objective and subjective reality. The reader should keep in mind, though, that this view is a matter of convenience; the view of a mystic would be very different.

PART II

HOW WE GOT HERE

Chapter 6
The Big Bang and the Origin of the Elements

Most people consider that the word 'evolution' solely describes a biological process. Indeed, when Young-Earth Creationists attack the teaching of evolution, they direct their attention to the curricula and textbooks of biology. However, the question of how humans came to populate this planet is a story that integrates the fields of biology with geology, chemistry, physics and astronomy. This is why scientists of all disciplines react strongly to the attempts of Creationists and supporters of Intelligent Design to instill their views on the teaching of 'science'. Thus, before we can discuss the metaphysical implications of evolution, we must understand the scientific story of how we got here.

As with all societies, Western science has developed its own story for the origin of the Earth and all the beings on it. Unlike the story in the Book of Genesis, which Young-Earth Creationists present as fact, the scientific story of how we got here is a theory that has grown over the past century-and-a-half due to the accumulation of facts and observations in many fields of science. Almost certainly, 100 years from now the scientific story of how we got here will be different than it is today, for it will have evolved to be consistent with a growing amount of information. Creationists consider this a great weakness, because scientists can never be certain that all the details in the story we tell of how we got here are true. Most scientists, however, argue that this is the strength of science. Every theory presented in science is subject to continual revision and for this reason we can be certain that what we put forth today fits the existing data better than any other competing theory. The scientific story of genesis is not simply a biological one. To get a full picture of how the Earth and the life we see upon it formed, one must also rely upon physics, chemistry, astronomy and geology. In the next five chapters I present the scientific story of genesis and show how much it relies on sciences other than biology. In doing this, I will try to furnish as much of the data as possible to show the reasoning through which the theory was constructed.

The Red Shift and the Big Bang Theory

One of the great discoveries of modern physics was that, when elements are heated to high temperatures, they emit light of a fixed set of wavelengths. We now know that this light is emitted when electrons within a heated atom jump from one energy level to another. Because each element has a distinct configuration of electrons, each element emits a different wavelength of light when excited. The first hint of this phenomenon was described in 1814 when a German scientist, Joseph von Fraunhofer, noticed a large number of wavelengths were missing in the light that is emitted from the sun. In other words, he discovered that the solar spectrum contains a number of strange black lines. He designated the darkest of these lines with letters of the alphabet. These dark lines were called Fraunhofer lines and their origin remained a mystery until 1859. At that time two German scientists, Robert Bunsen and Gustav Kirchoff, discovered that various types of metals emitted light of a distinct color when they were heated. When they heated sodium they noted that it emitted a bright yellow light that had the exact wavelength of one of the Fraunhofer lines. They concluded that absorption of light by sodium gas in the solar atmosphere produced the D line of Fraunhofer.

This exciting breakthrough meant that scientists could measure the chemical composition of the stars, even though they were millions and billions of kilometers (or miles) away. By the 1880s nearly fifty elements had been identified in the solar spectrum. One element, helium, which was named after the

Greek sun god Helios, was found on the sun before it was discovered on Earth.

In 1842, Christian Doppler of the University of Prague observed that a sound with a fixed frequency has a higher pitch if the object emitting it were moving toward the listener than if it were moving away. This has since been called the 'Doppler effect', and it explains why the sound of a race car or of a train whistle changes as the vehicle passes you. Doppler suggested that this effect would also affect light from the stars. Astronomers immediately tried to use the Doppler shift of the Fraunhofer lines in astral spectra to measure the velocity of the stars. They had a very difficult time doing this with the equipment available in the late nineteenth century, but by the beginning of the twentieth century equipment had improved to the point that astronomers were able to make a number of measurements.

By the 1920s it became clear that the spectra of all the stars were red shifted, i.e. they were moved to higher wavelengths. This meant that all the stars measured up to 1920 (and all the stars that have been measured since then) were moving away from us. In 1924, the German astronomer Carl Wirtz noted that the further away a star (or galaxy) was from us the greater is its velocity. In 1929 Edwin Hubble recognized a linear relation between the velocity of a star and its distance from Earth. This observation established Hubble's Law, which states that the further an astronomical object is from us the faster is its velocity. The rate of velocity increase was called Hubble's Constant.

If all the objects in the universe are moving away from us at a rate that increases with distance, it follows that all the objects were closer together in the past. This means that at some time in the distant past all the objects were clustered together in a mass that was incredibly dense. This observation lead to the Big Bang theory, which postulates that the universe began as a massive explosion, and has been expanding outward ever since. A few years ago NASA's Wilkinson Microwave Anisotropy Probe mapped the distribution of radiation left over from the Big Bang. By calculating how this distribution changed with time, astronomers were able to determine that the Big Bang occurred 13,700 million years ago; this is the accepted age of the universe.

The Origin of the Elements

Immediately after the Big Bang, the universe was so hot that even atoms didn't exist; in other words, there were no elements. Thus, all the elements and the vast array of chemical compounds that we have around us came into existence as the universe cooled from the Big Bang. Before we describe how this happened, we have to discuss the make-up of the elements. Each atom is composed of three 'elementary particles'[30]: the electron, which has very little mass and a negative charge; the proton, which has about 1800 times the mass of an electron and a positive charge, and a neutron, which has approximately the mass of a proton and no charge. The protons and neutrons are clustered in the nucleus that lies in the center of the atom whereas the electrons move around this nucleus at certain fixed energy levels.

Each element gets its distinctive chemical characteristics from the number of electrons that surround its nucleus and the energy levels that those electrons occupy. An element has a fixed number of electrons and protons, but it may have a variable number of neutrons. Because a neutron has no charge, the addition of a neutron to an atom increases its mass but does not affect its chemical properties. This means that an element of a given atomic number (which is the number of electrons or protons the atom contains) may have a range of atomic masses, depending on the number of neutrons present. These different masses of the same element are called *isotopes*. Isotopes are symbolized by prefixing the chemical symbol with the mass of the isotope. For example, hydrogen consisting of one proton and one electron would be symbolized ^{1}H; whereas hydrogen with one proton, one electron and one neutron, the isotope of hydrogen known as deuterium, would be ^2H.

Models of the Big Bang suggest that protons, neutrons and electrons began to form a few minutes after the birth of the universe, but that it took about 100,000 years for temperatures to cool enough for these particles to cluster into neutral atoms. This happened when a proton and an electron collided to produce hydrogen and the temperature was low enough so that the hydrogen would not decompose again into its constituent proton and electron. Collision of hydrogen atoms with additional electrons, protons and neutrons would have produced very minor amounts of helium and trace quantities of the light elements lithium and beryllium. There may have been a smattering of the heavier elements also present, but the chemistry of the early universe was immensely impoverished compared to what we are used to on Earth today.

Immediately after the Big Bang there were, of course, no stars and certainly no planets. For some reason (cosmologists have no idea why) the matter produced by the Big Bang, which was mostly hydrogen, was not distributed evenly through space. In some areas there was slightly more material than in others. Over time, the gas in the denser areas began coalescing under the pull of gravity. Eventually the gravitational attraction within this gas cloud became so intense that it forced two atoms of hydrogen and two neutrons together with enough velocity to make helium (Figure 7). When this happened, a proto-star was born. During the formation of helium, a small amount of mass was converted to energy according to Einstein's famous equation $E = mc^2$ (where E = energy emitted, m = mass, and c = speed of light). This process, which is the same one that occurs within the hydrogen bomb, produces immense amounts of energy. This energy, which appeared in the form of heat, would have caused the gas in the cloud to expand. Thus, there were two forces at work in our evolving protostar: gravity, which was causing the gas cloud to contract, and heating from nuclear reactions, which was causing it to expand. Eventually, when temperatures reached around 10 million degrees centigrade, the nuclear reactions became intense enough to balance the contraction of the gas cloud caused by gravity and a stable star was born.

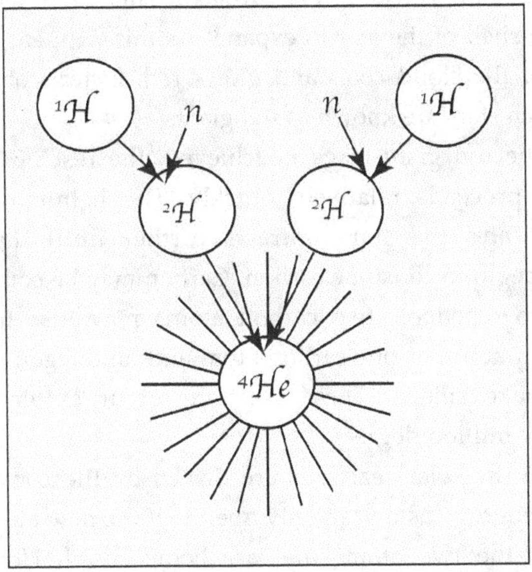

Figure 7 Diagram showing how helium (He) (and lots of energy) is probably produced within stars from hydrogen (H) and neutrons (n).

After a star forms, its evolution depends on its original mass. As the hydrogen in the star is converted to helium, the star becomes denser. This causes the interior of the star to contract and the temperature of the star's core to increase. Because the rate of hydrogen consumption depends on the intensity of the gravitational attraction, the lifetime of stars is dependent on their size. Small stars may burn hydrogen for several thousand million years, whereas large stars will deplete their fuel in only a few million years. Once hydrogen has been depleted, there is no longer enough heat generated by fusion to counteract contraction under the pull of gravity. The star then contracts until the temperature and pressure within it are sufficient to cause the fusion of helium. Helium may be consumed by two reactions: three helium atoms may combine to form one carbon atom, or four helium atoms may combine to make an oxygen atom. A star starts burning helium at about 100 million degrees centigrade, which is about ten times hotter than one consuming hydrogen. This high temperature causes the shell of the star to expand. As this happens, the outer margins of the cloud cools and glows red, instead of the usual yellow. Such stars are known as red giants.

Once the red giant stage is achieved, the rest of the stellar evolution proceeds relatively quickly. The helium is rapidly consumed and the star contracts further until the nuclear reactions begin to consume carbon. Carbon may be consumed by one of two reactions: two carbon atoms may fuse to make a magnesium atom, or one carbon atom and an oxygen atom may fuse to make silicon. These reactions occur at temperatures around 500 million degrees.

Because the solar reactions are driven by the conversion of mass into energy, fusion can only operate if the new atom has *less* mass than the two atoms that are being fused. However, as elements get heavier they contain increasingly more neutrons relative to the electrons and protons. This means that atoms heavier than iron (atomic mass 57) cannot be produced by fusion because they are *more* massive (in the form of additional neutrons) than any combination of atoms that may form them. Because elements heavier than iron cannot form by fusion of lighter elements, once a star has depleted its light elements, the nuclear reaction within its core will shut off. When this happens, there is no longer any force to withstand the contraction of gravity and the star collapses. If the star is relatively small, the contraction will produce a dense dead star known as a brown dwarf. However, if the star is large enough, the gravitational attraction within the core becomes so great that the contraction becomes explosive. The resulting explosion, which is known as a supernova, blows the star to pieces and spews its remnants into surrounding space.

Cosmologists postulate that those heavy elements that cannot be formed by fusion are produced by neutron bombardment in stars. For example, during neutron bombardment ^{57}Fe may absorb a neutron to become ^{58}Fe (Figure 8A). ^{58}Fe is a stable isotope of iron; so the net effect of this reaction is only to change the mass of an iron atom. However, if ^{57}Fe absorbs two neutrons it becomes ^{59}Fe, which is not stable. Eventually one of the neutrons in this isotope will break down to an electron and a proton. The breakdown of a neutron in ^{59}Fe changes the number of protons in the nucleus and, hence produces a new element ^{59}Co, a stable isotope of cobalt (Figure 8B). This reaction releases a lot of energy, causing the electron produced by this reaction to be expelled from the atom as a high-energy particle and leaving the cobalt behind as a positively charged ion. This process is known as *fission* and is the process that produces the radioactivity in some heavy elements such as uranium or radium.

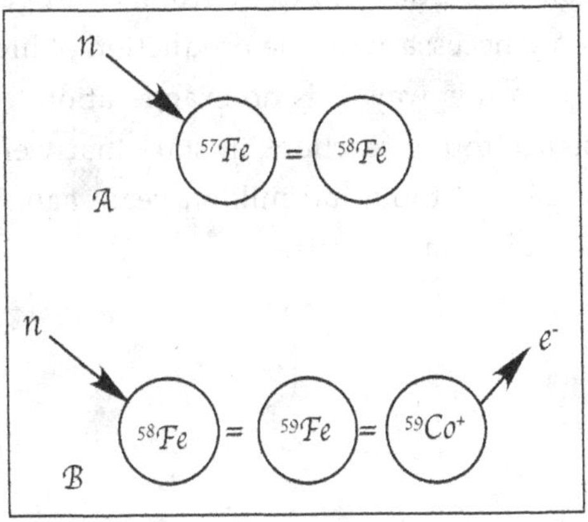

Figure 8 Diagram showing the effects of neutron bombardment on atoms within a star. A. Absorption of a neutron turns a stable isotope of an element into another stable isotope. B. Bombardment forms an unstable isotope that eventually decays to a stable isotope of another, heavier element.

Although the production of heavy elements by neutron bombardment occurs to some extent within stable stars, cosmologists maintain that most of the heavy elements were produced in supernovae. The explosion of heavy stars produces a huge dose of neutrons that react with the iron and other elements in the star to form an array of very heavy isotopes. Most of these isotopes are unstable and as they are radiated into space with the debris of the supernova, they decay to produce all the heavy elements in the periodic table. Some isotopes are so unstable that they decay away in a matter of minutes, others, such as uranium, take hundreds of millions of years to break down, which explains why a large number of radioactive isotopes still occur naturally.

Throughout the life of the universe, countless stars have formed, grown old and then died in supernova explosions. In the process, they produced all the elements that we are familiar with, such as carbon, oxygen, iron, copper, and lead. Generation after generation of stars were born, consumed hydrogen and helium in nuclear reactions, and then blew the resulting heavy elements into space from supernovae. Apart from hydrogen, all of the elements that are necessary for the production of life as we know it were formed in this way. It is no exaggeration to say that we owe our existence to the reactions in stars that were obliterated by explosions several thousand million years ago. We are quite literally, produced from stardust.

Chapter 7
The Origin of the Earth

One of the major points of dispute the Creationists have about the theory of evolution is the age of the Earth. Creationists may not necessarily accept that the Earth was created on October 22, 4004 B.C., as postulated by the Irish cleric Bishop Usher in 1656, but they hold that the age of the Earth is measured in thousands, rather than thousands of millions of years. Geologists have long considered that this age is far too young. In 1785 James Hutton, in his book, *Theory of the Earth,* argued that the geologic processes we see operating today are the same that operated in the past. If this were so, then it would have taken an immense amount of time to wear down the folded mountains he saw in Scotland and to cover them with thick accumulations of sediments. Although the first geologists knew the Earth was old, it took more than 150 years for geologists to determine just how long a period of time was involved.[31]

Throughout the 19th century scientists tried various ways to estimate the age of the Earth. Perhaps the most compelling method was to calculate how long it would take a molten body the size of the Earth to cool. This is the approach used by Lord Kelvin, a professor of Natural Philosophy at the University of Glasgow and probably the foremost British scientist of the latter half of the nineteenth century. In 1862, based on many assumptions about the original temperature of the Earth and the parameters governing its cooling rate, he estimated that the Earth was between 20 million and 400 million years old. In 1897 he refined this estimate to 20 to 40 million years. Many geologists disputed these estimates because they seemed to belie the geologic evidence of an ancient Earth. Darwin's theory of evolution, of course, figured prominently in this dispute, because if the Earth was as young as Lord Kelvin had estimated there wouldn't have been enough time for all the species on the planet to evolve.

The dispute over Lord Kelvin's age of the Earth lasted for most of the latter nineteenth century and then died suddenly, just as the 20th century dawned. In 1903 two British scientists, Ernest Rutherford and Frederick Soddy (both of whom were later to win Noble Prizes), published a paper noting that the newly discovered phenomenon of radioactivity produces a vast amount of heat. The availability of a previously unrecognized source of heat immediately killed Lord Kelvin's model for the age of the Earth.

In his calculations, Lord Kelvin assumed that all the heat in the Earth today was produced by meteorite impacts during the formation of our planet and that, once the meteorite impacts ceased, heat from the Earth has been radiating into space. This model, elegant though it was, suffered from the same problem that plagued the blind men who were arguing about the nature of the elephant; it was missing one crucial piece of data. As soon as Rutherford and Soddy showed that radioactive processes within the Earth produce a large amount of heat, Lord Kelvin's model fell apart and the last scientific argument for a young Earth (though Lord Kelvin's age estimate was much, much older that Biblical estimates) evaporated. The discovery of radioactivity also provided a way for scientists to calculate an absolute age for the Earth and the Solar system, though it took nearly fifty years for geologists to fully exploit this technique.

How Isotopic Clocks Work

As we noted in the previous chapter, many elements with high atomic weights are radioactive. From time to time an atom of one of these elements spontaneously decays to a different element by emitting charged particles. This is not a random process; the decay of each radioactive parent isotope to a stable daughter isotope follows a distinct path and occurs at a statistically reliable rate. This rate is known as the half-life of an isotope. After one half-life, half of the parent would have decayed to the daughter.

After another half-life, half of the remaining parent atoms would have decayed. Thus, after two half-lives only 1/4 of the parent would remain. After eight half-lives more than 99.5% of the parent would have decayed away.

Because the abundance of a daughter element grows as the parent decays (Figure 9A), all one needs to do to define a geologic clock from a given isotopic system is to compare the abundances of a parent isotope to that of the daughter isotope. The ratio of the abundances of the two isotopes is a function of the number of half-lives that have elapsed since the clock began keeping time (Figure 9B). For example, if the daughter element is 15 times more abundant than the parent, the system has been evolving for 4 half-lives of the parent.

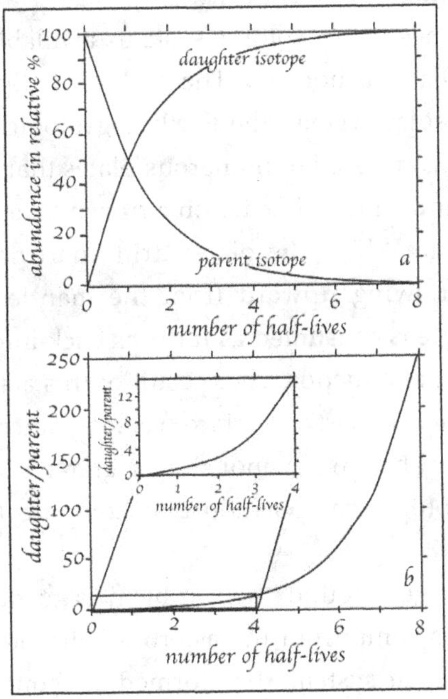

Figure 9 Diagram showing the relative abundances of parent and daughter isotopes as a function of the number of half-lives elapsed. b. Diagram showing the ratio of daughter to parent as a function of the number of half-lives elapsed.

The Age of the Earth

Over the past decades, geochemists have recognized four isotopic systems – potassium (K)-argon (Ar), rubidium (Rb)-strontium (Sr), samarium (Sm)-neodymium (Nd), and uranium (U)-lead (Pb) – that can serve as chronometers for studying the evolution of the Earth and the solar system (in each of the systems mentioned above, the first element is the parent and the second is the daughter). Each of these isotopic systems has a half-life of the right duration so that a measurable amount of both the parent and daughter isotope can be found even in the oldest rocks. Each system contains elements that have different geochemical behavior so that application of more than one isotopic system to the study of a rock or suite of rocks tells the geochemist much about the evolution of those rocks.

Even with these four isotopic systems available, determining the age of the Earth is not easy. The problem is that, unlike other planets in the solar system, the Earth is geologically active. The Earth's crust is composed of numerous plates that float above the underlying mantle; much like ice on a frozen lake floats upon the water beneath it. Where the plates drift apart new crust forms from magma flowing upward from the mantle. Where plates collide, one plate is consumed as it drops back into the mantle in a process called subduction. As a result of this activity, all of the original crust on the Earth's surface has long since been recycled into the mantle. Thus, we cannot simply grab a sample of a rock, measure its isotopic composition and compute the age of the Earth.

One way to get around this problem is to date meteorites. Most meteorites come from the asteroid belt and, because they are part of the solar system, they formed at about the same time as the Earth. Furthermore, most meteorites have not been subjected to later heating or deformation that could let daughter isotopes escape. Hence, the isotopic clocks within them record the time at which they (and by analogy, the Earth) formed. Figure

10 shows that the four different isotopic systems described above all give ages of more than 4000 million years for meteorites, with a maximum around 4500 million. There is a smattering of younger ages. Ages as young as 1000 million are reported, but those younger ages are from meteorites that have been subjected to later deformation. Hence their age is considered to reflect the date of deformation of the rock, not its formation.

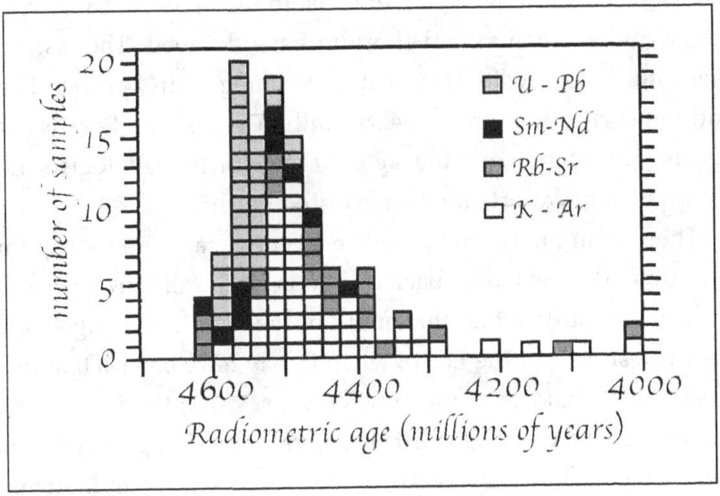

Figure 10 Histogram showing the radiometric ages for meteorites as measured by four different isotopic systems [32].

Unlike meteorites, rocks from Earth show a wide spectrum of ages. The youngest crust on Earth comes from the ocean floor, only small portions of which are more than 100 million years old. The continents contain rocks with a wide range of ages, with modern volcanic regions obviously being very young. Most continents contain areas of rocks that were formed around 2500 million years ago and in a few places around the world there are rocks that are 3300 to 4030 million years old. Grains of the uranium-bearing mineral zircon as old as 4400 million years old have been found in some ancient sandstones, but, as yet, few rocks more than 4000 million years old been found on Earth.

One way to get around this problem of dating the Earth is to assume that all of the uranium and lead on Earth come from a common reservoir. Lead consists of four major isotopes. Of these, two are produced by radioactive decay of uranium, one by radioactive breakdown of the element thorium, and one, known as 'common lead', is not produced by radioactive decay of any element. Over time, the abundance of common lead has remained the same while the radiogenic isotopes have become more abundant as uranium and thorium have decayed. The last time the isotopic composition of lead was homogenous between Earth and meteorites was around 4560 million years ago. Because this age is consistent with the ages of meteorites, geologists now accept it as the approximate age of the Earth.

There is an interesting paradox when we talk about deep time (i.e. time that extends back millions and millions of years). Scientists postulate that the length of the year has changed since the earliest days of the Earth, when it may have been 400 or more days long. What do we mean when we say that the Earth is 4560 million years old, if the length of the year has changed over time? What's worse, how can we say the universe is 13700 million years old when, for the first 9250 million years there was no Earth (and no sun) and, hence a year, which is defined as a single revolution of the Earth around the sun, cannot be defined? The answer to this is that most of these calculations are done in terms of seconds. Half-lives are determined experimentally in nuclear reactors and are measured in terms the number of particles that decay per second. The calculations on the age of the universe were done using the velocity of the various stars, which is measured in kilometers per second. Seconds are defined by the periodicity of the radiation from an isotope of cesium (^{123}Cs) and this definition is valid even at a time when the Earth and the sun didn't exist. To help people visualize the huge expanse of geologic and cosmologic time, scientists convert the age in seconds to the duration of a modern year (1 year = 365 days =

31,536,000 seconds). This allows a year to be defined when talking about extremely old events, even if the amount of time it took the Earth to circle the sun back then was different from what it is today, or if neither the Earth nor the sun even existed.

The Geologic Time Scale

Even though the advent of geochronology allows us to put an absolute age on most geologic events, when discussing the evolution of life it is advantageous to use the geologic time scale (Figure 11). Geologists established the major components of the time scale 150 years ago, long before they had any way to append isotopic ages to it. Despite its antiquity, the geologic time scale is still handy when discussing evolution because it is based directly upon the changes that are seen in the fossil record. In the early 19th century, as geology began to develop into a new field of science, geologists endeavored to correlate strata across Europe by comparing the fossils found within each sequence. They found that various strata contain distinctive fossil assemblages and that these assemblages changed, often abruptly, from layer to layer. To establish the geologic time scale, geologists assumed that strata containing the same assemblage of fossils were deposited during the same interval and that rock layers lying lower in a stratigraphic section are older than those that are above them. Isotopic ages were added much later with the development of radiometric dating.

The fundamental division in the geologic time scale lies at around 545 million years ago, at the beginning of the Cambrian period, when abundant fossil shells appear in the geologic record. This event separates the geologic time scale into two unequal periods. The younger period, when sedimentary rocks are characterized by a record of fossilized hard parts, is called the Phanerozoic (which means 'obvious life'). In the older one, the Precambrian, readily visible fossils are scarce and, where present, are restricted to individual cells, cell colonies, or traces.

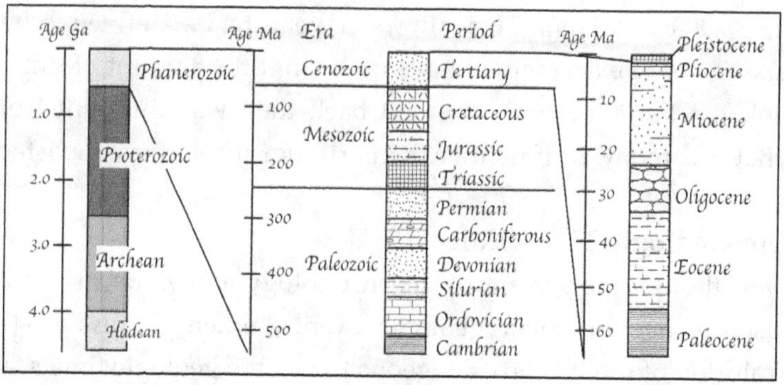

Figure 11 Geologic time scale. Ma = mega annum (millions of years), Ga = giga annum (1000s of millions of years).

The presence of fossils has allowed geologists to subdivide the Phanerozoic time scale in great detail (Figure. 11). It is divided into three broad eras: the Paleozoic, roughly the time before the dinosaurs; the Mesozoic, (commonly known as the 'age of dinosaurs'), and the Cenozoic, (commonly known as the 'age of mammals'). The Precambrian has been divided into three ages: the Proterozoic, the Archean, and the Hadean. The division between the Archean and the Proterozoic has been established at 2.5 billon years ago, partially because there is a distinct lack of rocks of this age throughout North America and Europe. The Hadean is the name given to the interval of Earth's history before there is a geologic record, roughly from 4500 to 4000 million years ago.

The Origin of the Solar System

In 1776, Marquis de Laplace proposed that the sun and the solar system surrounding it formed by condensation of a rotating cloud of gas. Perhaps the strongest evidence for this is the fact that all the planets in the solar system revolve around the sun in the same direction and lie approximately on the same plane. If the planets had been pre-existing bodies that were captured as they wandered by the sun, their orbits should have random orientations.

The present model, which is far more sophisticated than that put forth by Laplace, goes like this: About 4600 million years ago a dust cloud in our neighborhood of the galaxy began to collapse under the power of its own gravity. Some cosmologists contend that the explosion of a nearby supernova may have triggered this collapse. The vast majority of the material in the cloud (which consisted of approximately 99% hydrogen and helium and 1% of the rest of the elements) settled into the star that was growing in the center of the cloud. The rest of this material formed a nebula that rotated in a disk around the star. As the protosun began to develop, the heat it produced drove the volatile components in the surrounding cloud out to the outer portions of the nebula. This produced a compositional zoning that was retained in the planets that later coalesced from the cloud. As a result of this zoning, the planets that formed closest to the sun (Mercury, Venus, Earth, and Mars) are depleted in the lightest elements and consist mostly of oxygen, silicon, iron, and magnesium. These inner rocky planets may have an atmosphere, but it is thin. The lighter elements (hydrogen, helium, carbon, nitrogen, oxygen and sulfur) are concentrated in outer planets (Jupiter, Saturn, Uranus and Neptune). These are giant gaseous bodies that may not have any rocky core.

As with other planets in the solar system, the Earth grew out of the nebula by accreting matter from the general vicinity of its orbit. Most of the material that fell into the Earth in this process was made of meteorites known as chondrites. Chondrites consist of an agglomeration of particles that were cemented together in space without melting. Although geochemists think that the Earth formed from chondritic meteorites, there are few rocks on Earth that have a chondritic composition. This is because the heat generated by accretion of meteorites caused the early Earth to melt. As this melt cooled, the denser elements, such as iron and nickel sank into the core. Lighter elements such as silica and magnesium were enriched in the overlying mantle, whereas the lightest elements, such as aluminum and sodium were concentrated in a thin, light crust that floats like foam on the denser mantle. When this process, known as differentiation, occurred has been one of the key questions in geology.

The answer to this question came from the lunar rocks that were brought back to Earth by the Apollo missions. Astronomers now believe that the moon was formed when a Mars-sized meteor struck the Earth. The impact caused extensive melting in the Earth's mantle and propelled much of it into space. Some of this material fell back to Earth, but a good proportion of it assembled itself in orbit around the Earth to form the moon. The oldest radiometric age obtained from the Moon is 4510 million years. This means that the collision that formed the moon occurred approximately 50 million years after the accretion of the Earth. The moon has a distinctly lower bulk metal content than the Earth, which leads geochemists to conclude that differentiation and the sequestration of the metals into the core of the Earth had happened within a few tens of millions of years of Earth's history, before the formation of the moon.

An important geochemical characteristic of the Earth is that it contains two distinct types of crust. The basaltic crust of the ocean basins is about 10% denser than the granitic crust of the continents. Both of these 'float' on a dense mantle that is plastic enough to allow this density difference to be reflected topographically. Because of its lower density, granitic crust floats about 4 to 5 kilometers (2.5 to 3 miles) higher than the oceanic crust. Because of their different densities, these types of crust have had very different histories. The oceanic crust is dense enough so it is easily recycled into the mantle by subduction, whereas the less dense granitic crust is only rarely subducted. This means that the continents drift around the surface of the Earth among an oceanic crust that is continually being consumed and regenerated. This explains why the oldest rocks on Earth are found on the continents, whereas the rocks of the ocean basins are relatively young.

Although geologists have yet to find many rocks older than 4000 million years old, recent isotopic studies indicate that substantial crustal differentiation occurred as early as 4460 million years ago and that the early Earth and modern Earth had similar abundances of continental crust. This earliest crust must have been thoroughly recycled into the mantle via meteorite bombardment or subduction. Only around 4000 million years ago did the cosmic bombardment of Earth slow down enough to allow the preservation of the crust.

The Origin of the Atmosphere

Another major question in the history of our planet is how did the atmosphere form? The collision that produced the moon 4510 million years ago probably also blew away whatever atmosphere surrounded the early planet. Therefore, the atmosphere that you and I breathe today must have accumulated since then. Traditionally, geologists have concluded that the atmosphere was produced from volcanic gases emitted from the mantle during the long history of the Earth. Modern volcanoes emit a large amount of gas, mostly carbon dioxide and water. It is likely that early in the Earth's history an even greater amount of gases was emitted from volcanoes. This is partially because there was a much higher rate of volcanic activity and partially because the mantle was probably richer in volatile components in the past than it is today. These gases emitted from the volcanoes were held close to the planet by the Earth's gravity and eventually accumulated to make the oceans and atmosphere.

Recently it has been proposed that the atmosphere could have been carried to Earth by comets. Comets are clots of cosmic ice that contain important amounts of carbon, nitrogen, and sulfur, as well as water. They probably formed by accretion from the nebulitic cloud in the outer reaches of the solar system, where these elements were relatively abundant. Most of the icy material in the outer solar system was swept up during the accretion of the giant planets (Jupiter, Saturn, Uranus and Neptune). Some of the comets that survived the accretion would have missed direct impact with one the great planets. As they sped by the planet the gravitational pull of the planet may have flung the comet into an entirely new orbit, some of which could have brought comets toward the inner solar system. A small proportion of those comets that invaded the inner solar system could have collided with the Earth and brought the volatile components that make up our oceans and atmosphere.

The Composition of the Early Atmosphere

If you had visited the Earth shortly after the meteorite bombardment ceased, you would have found it to be a hellish place indeed. The atmosphere contained very little free oxygen and, without substantial oxygen, there would be no ozone (O_3) in the upper atmosphere. Ozone absorbs ultraviolet light from space; without the ozone shield, the surface of the planet would be scorched by withering ultraviolet radiation. To move about in this environment we would have needed protective suits that are not very different from those used by astronauts in outer space. Encased in a space suit, our excursion on Earth would have revealed a very unpleasant world. The interaction between the ultraviolet light and the CO_2-rich atmosphere probably produced thick smog. This, when added to the dust that swirled in the winds of the thick atmosphere, meant that even on a 'clear' day the sun and the moon (which was much closer then, and hence would have appeared much bigger than it does today) were probably veiled by clouds. The surface of the planet consisted of black or grey rock decorated with pockets of white sand or dust. Under this smoggy atmosphere the oceans had a dreary grey appearance. The air temperature may have been extremely hot, perhaps near the boiling temperature of water, and because of the thick cloud cover; the temperature probably didn't vary much between day and night. Only a few minutes on the surface of this hellish planet would convince you that this place had very poor prospects for hosting life.

How close to truth is the scenario presented above, or to put it another way, how is it that geochemists can determine the composition of the atmosphere that covered the early Earth? After all, as the Creationists say, there was no one around to see it so how do we know it occurred? Clearly any trace of the early atmosphere has long since disappeared. We cannot know the composition of the early atmosphere for certain, but geochemists can make some good inferences. First off, we can be relatively sure that the early atmosphere consisted mostly of the elements nitrogen, carbon, oxygen, and hydrogen, since they are the major constituents of the atmosphere today. These elements, however, can be combined to produce many possible gases. Oxygen could have occurred as a free gas (O_2) or could have been entirely bound to hydrogen to make water (H_2O) and with carbon to make carbon dioxide (CO_2) or carbon monoxide (CO). Hydrogen could occur as a free gas (H_2) or could be totally bounded to oxygen as H_2O, to nitrogen as ammonia (NH_3), or to carbon as methane (CH_4). Exactly which gases were present in the early atmosphere depends on the relative abundances of H_2 and O_2. If the atmosphere was oxidizing (that is, if it had a good deal of free oxygen, as it does today), then all the hydrogen would have been bound to oxygen to make water, the atmosphere would have consisted of N_2, O_2, H_2O, and CO_2, and there would have been vanishingly small amounts of the hydrogenated gases (NH_4 and CH_4). If the atmosphere were highly reducing (i.e. it contained large amounts of free H_2 rather than O_2), then nitrogen and carbon in the atmosphere would have been bound to hydrogen to make NH_4 and CH_4.

Geochemists estimate the composition of the early atmosphere by determining what rocks were likely to have been exposed on the Earth's surface. We can then use chemical thermodynamics to calculate the partial pressure of oxygen that would be in equilibrium with these rocks and from that determine the abundances of the other gases. The first calculations like this assumed that the Earth's first atmosphere would have been in equilibrium with native iron, which is common in meteorites. Such an atmosphere would have been very reducing and would have consisted mostly of H_2, CH_4, perhaps with lesser amounts of NH_4, and H_2O. When lunar science showed that the moon was ejected from the Earth *after* the free metal in the Earth had already settled into the core, this picture changed. Geochemists now believe that the early atmosphere was in equilibrium with a much more oxidized rock, probably something similar to the basalts that are being erupted on Hawaii today. The gases emitted from the Hawaiian volcanoes are reduced (i.e. they contain no free oxygen), but they are not so reduced that large amounts of CH_4 and NH_4 are stable. If the early crust had been made up of basalt (which is very likely), then an atmosphere in equilibrium with it would have consisted of mostly CO_2 and N_2, with minor amounts of H_2O.

Nitrogen does not enter into many minerals, so the nitrogen content of the early atmosphere was probably pretty much like it is today. The CO_2 pressure of the early atmosphere is unknown, but it certainly was much higher than the 0.00036 bars that it is today. The abundance of CO_2 in the atmosphere is important because carbon dioxide is a greenhouse gas. It absorbs infrared light, and hence inhibits the Earth's heat from radiating into space. The more CO_2 in a planet's atmosphere, the less efficiently heat is radiated into space, and the warmer the planet will be.

The CO_2 content of the Earth's atmosphere is controlled by the interplay of several reactions. Before the advent of the Industrial Revolution, CO_2 was mainly added to the atmosphere through volcanic activity. Carbon dioxide is extracted from the atmosphere by the sequestering of carbon into organic matter or by weathering of silicates, which causes carbon to dissolve into water as a carbonate ion. The carbon dioxide content of the atmosphere, therefore, is a function of the complex interaction between CO_2 production by volcanoes (and more recently by humans) and its consumption by biological activity and weathering. Changes in the CO_2 content of the atmosphere are dampened by these reactions through a complex feedback mechanism. Increases in CO_2 are compensated by increases in weathering rates and biologic activity, which will increase the rate at which carbon dioxide is extracted from the atmosphere. In contrast, decreasing CO_2 in the atmosphere will cause a decrease in biological activity and weathering rates, decreasing its extraction rate from the atmosphere.

Although these feedback mechanisms slow down the rate at which the CO_2 content of the atmosphere changes, atmospheric CO_2 has varied greatly over time in response to long-term changes in the area of exposed rock, the abundance of life, and volcanic activity. For example, the past twenty million years has been a period of unusually intense mountain building as collisions between plates produced the Alps, the Himalayas, and Cordillera of North and South America. The exposure of vast amounts of rock in these mountains has lead to high weathering rates, which has depleted carbon dioxide from the atmosphere, causing CO_2 content of the present atmosphere to be lower now than it has been during most of geologic time. As a result, the present time is one of the few periods in Earth's history when the planet has supported glaciers.

Back in the earliest days of the Earth, there was no organic activity to extract carbon dioxide from the atmosphere. This means that the CO_2 could only be extracted from the atmosphere by weathering. If, as suggested above, the continents of the early Earth had a volume similar to what we find today, then CO_2 may have been extracted from the atmosphere by weathering at approximately the same rate as it is today. However, because the Earth contained more radioactive isotopes and suffered a higher impact rate from meteorites, the early Earth must have been hotter and more volcanically active than it is today. Therefore, input of CO_2 into the atmosphere was probably much higher than it is today. This suggests that the CO_2 content of the atmosphere was high; some authors have suggested that it may have had pressures as high as 10 bars (more than 10,000 times higher than it is today). In a way this was good for the origin of life because the young sun was about 20% cooler than it is now. If the atmosphere had not been CO_2-rich, the early Earth would have been too cold to support liquid water. Some authors maintain that the CO_2 content of the atmosphere was just high enough to keep the surface temperature of the Earth above freezing but most workers in the field contend that the Earth was much warmer, and that the early oceans had temperatures of 55°C to 85°C (131° to 185°F).

Chapter 8
The 'Tree' of Life

Life on our planet shows an amazing variety of forms and shapes but all living beings share two common features: they have a metabolism and they reproduce. Living creatures possess a metabolism that extracts energy from light or other nutrients in the surroundings, and they have a process that allows them to produce offspring that are nearly identical to the parents. In addition, though Creationists dispute this point, living species change with time.

Metabolism

Metabolism is a word describing the complex series of reactions whereby all living beings produce the energy and compounds necessary for the maintenance of life. Three of the most important compounds involved in metabolism are carbohydrates, amino acids, and proteins. Carbohydrates are complex compounds, such as sugar and starch that are constructed entirely of carbon, hydrogen and oxygen. Amino acids are organic compounds that, in addition to carbon hydrogen, and oxygen, contain nitrogen in the form of an amino group (NH_3). Amino acids form the basis of proteins, which are complex molecules that form the building blocks for organic tissue.

In the middle of the 19th Century, Louis Pasteur discovered that each amino acid occurs in two forms, depending on how the HN_3 radical is arranged on the molecule. One form will rotate polarized light to the right; the other rotates it to the left. A solution of amino acids made in the lab will consist of equal mixtures of right- and left-handed forms and it will not affect polarized light. Pasteur discovered that, in contrast to amino acids made in the lab, those extracted from organic compounds all rotate polarized light to the left. The reason for this has become one of the great mysteries of life.

The key reaction within metabolism is respiration, wherein living organisms produce carbohydrates from CO_2 and H_2O in the atmosphere. The simplest reaction we can write to model respiration is:

$$CO_2 + H_2O = H_2CO + O_2 \quad (1)$$

where H_2CO is formaldehyde, the simplest hydrocarbon.

Of course respiration doesn't produce formaldehyde, which is poisonous to most life, but H_2CO is the building block for more complex carbohydrates. Reaction (1) demonstrates how the production of any carbohydrate consumes carbon dioxide and water and produces oxygen gas. Somehow, living organisms combine H_2O and CO_2 via reaction (1) to make carbohydrates. Because we don't see water and carbon dioxide in our glass of soda spontaneously combining to make carbohydrates like alcohol, it is clear that an input of energy is needed to make these reactions proceed.

Life has evolved many strategies to obtain the energy needed to make carbohydrates (Table 2). Most people are aware that plants extract energy from sunlight, whereas animals cannot survive without eating plants or some other animals. Plants use energy from sunlight to run reaction (1) to the right, producing carbohydrates with oxygen as a waste product. Animals run reaction (1) in reverse, converting carbohydrates plus oxygen into energy plus water and CO_2. Organisms, like plants, that extract energy from their surroundings, are called *autotrophic,* which means 'self feeders'. Creatures that cannot do this are *heterotrophs,* because they are 'other feeders'.

Table 2 Metabolic mechanisms		
Autotrophs manufacture their own food		Heterotrophs get energy from others
Chemoautotrophs: get energy from chemical reactions	Photoautotrophs: get energy from light	
Chemolithoautotrophs: get energy from reactions involving rocks.		
Anerobic	Mostly aerobic	Mostly aerobic

The autotrophs that we are most familiar with are plants, which use chlorophyll to extract energy from sunlight. Autotrophs such as these are called *photoautotrophs*. A large variety of simpler life forms obtain the needed energy using reducing chemical compounds in the environment, including hydrogen, hydrogen sulfide, ferrous iron, and ammonia. Such creatures are called *chemoautotrophs*. Some chemoautotrophs extract energy directly from chemicals in the surrounding water, whereas others extract their energy by reactions involving minerals. Those creatures that 'eat rocks' are called *chemolithoautotrophs*.

Because we (and our favorite pets) are *aerobic* creatures (which means that we would die without access to free oxygen) most of us assume that oxygen is necessary for life. However that doesn't apply to chemoautotrophs. Because the compounds that chemoautotrophs need for energy are oxidized by free oxygen, these creatures are *anerobic*; to them oxygen is a poison.

Reproduction

When Darwin put forth his theory of natural selection he knew nothing about how parents pass their traits on to their offspring. The fact that science didn't fully understand this process of inheritance until nearly a century after the publication of *The Origin of The Species*, speaks volumes about the prescience of

Darwin's theory. In 1866, shortly after the publication of Darwin's book, the monk, Gregor Mendel, published his classic work on a long series of experiments he had conducted on inheritance in peas. Although the work was overlooked for years, Mendel's research formed the groundwork for the science that was later to be known as genetics. From his experiments, Mendel concluded that 'particles of inheritance' resided in both the male and female generative parts of his plants. These 'particles of inheritance' were later called genes, but it took nearly a century before scientists could determine what genes are and how they operate.

In the early years of the Twentieth Century, biologists recognized that chromosomes, thread-like structures within cells, seem to duplicate whenever a cell divides. In cells with the larger chromosomes, biologists could see genes strung out along the chromosome like beads on a string. In the 1920s, scientists established that the chromosomes were composed of proteins and a substance called deoxyribonucleic acid (known among its friends as DNA). Further experiments showed that it was the DNA that carried the genetic information. The major question was: How did DNA manage to transfer this information from one generation to the next?

The answer came in 1953 when James Watson and Frances Crick unraveled the structure of DNA. They showed that DNA consists of a double chain of carbon atoms that are twisted together into a spiral and are bound together by four nucleotides: adenine, guanine, cytosine, and thymine. These are commonly abbreviated as A, G, C, and T. The whole genetic variation of life depends on how these four nucleotides are arranged on the DNA chain. The secret of DNA is that A can only bind to T and C can only bind to G (Figure 12). This means that each chain in a DNA molecule contains all the information that is encoded within the original double helix. Thus, when a cell divides, the DNA coil splits into two chains. Each chain can construct a new DNA coil from nutrients within the cell while retaining all the genetic information that was encoded in the original cell.

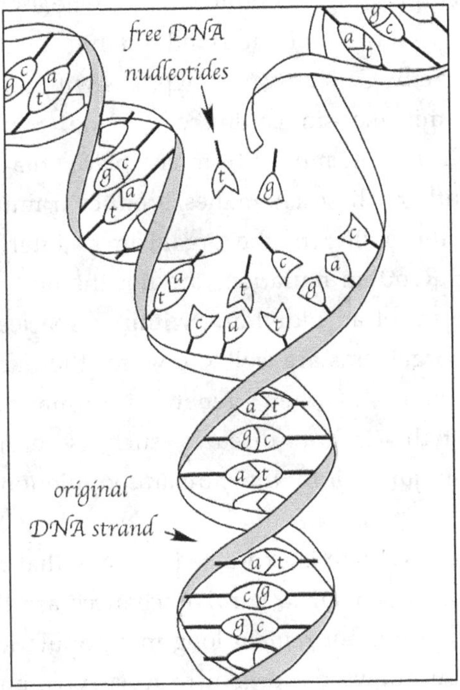

Figure 12 Diagram showing the reproduction of one double strand of DNA into two double strands. A = adenine, G = guanine, C = cytosine, and T = thymine.

The DNA within a cell is relatively inert with respect to metabolic processes. The heavy lifting for this job goes to another complex organic molecule called RNA (ribonucleic acid). Transfer RNA (or tRNA) takes the genetic message that is coded within the DNA and transfers it to the ribosomes, where metabolism of proteins takes place. There, ribosomal RNA (or rRNA) takes these codes (in the forms of the nucleotides A, C, G, and T) and uses them when forming the proteins necessary for the operation of the cell.

Evolution

Not only did the discovery of DNA's structure lead to the explanation of how genes carry information within organisms; it also provided a key to understanding how some important aspects of evolution occur. During reproduction, the whole genome, which can run into hundreds of thousands of bits of data, must be duplicated exactly. Generally, this happens with no problem, but occasionally mistakes in coding are made. Some genes are deleted, duplicated, or moved from one place on a chromosomal strand to another. These anomalies produce a mutation, which may change the ability of the organism to interface with the environment. Random mutations are not the only way that the genetic make up of an individual within a species can change. Single-celled organisms are well known for their ability to swap large components of their genetic information. Scientists postulate that this is how diseases, such as certain strains of influenza, can jump into the human population from other species.

If the genetic change is expressed in traits that make it more difficult for an organism to survive, chances are that this new genetic makeup will not remain long in a population. However, if the mutation allows the organism to survive and reproduce more readily than other members of the species, then this new genetic information will be passed on to its offspring. Genetic changes may propagate through a species with amazing rapidity, particularly if the species is under stress. A good example of this is the disease tuberculosis. TB was a feared disease until the middle of the twentieth century when antibiotic drugs were discovered. Very quickly tuberculosis was converted from a killer to an easily treated disease and its occurrence within the human population went into a steep decline. Unfortunately, within the past few years antibiotic-resistant strains of the disease have evolved that are much more difficult to treat. As a result, an increasing number of drug-resistant cases of tuberculosis have been reported worldwide and TB is on the verge of becoming the dreaded killer it was a century ago.

Although individual mutations may be produced by random

changes in the genetic code, the path of evolution is far from random. There are a limited number of ways that organisms can 'solve' an evolutionary problem and it is clear that organisms have settled upon these ways many times during the history of evolution. This process is called convergence. Consider a shark, a porpoise and an *Ichthyosaurus*. For those of you who did not have a childhood fascination for dinosaurs and didn't learn what an *Ichthyosaurus* was as a child, I enclose a picture of one in Figure 13. Each of these animals looks like a fish, with a streamlined body, flippers, and fins. The problem is that only the shark is a fish. The *Ichthyosaurus* is an extinct reptile, and the porpoise is a mammal. Both the *Ichthyosaurus* and the porpoise evolved from land-based creatures that returned to the sea.[33] The most efficient way for an animal to move through the water is for it to have a streamlined body that is propelled with flat, paddle-like flippers. Thus, it is not surprising that under the pressures of natural selection, the bodies of the precursors to the *Ichthyosaurus* and the porpoises became more streamlined and their limbs became more paddle-like, until they had attained the appearance of the fish they hunt.

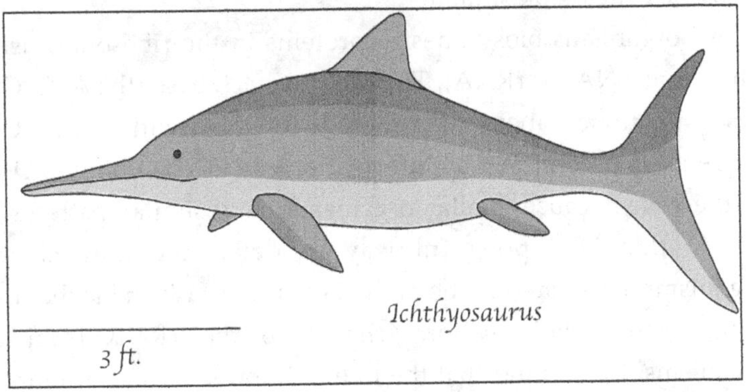

Figure 13 *Ichthyosaurus*, a marine reptile that lived 245 – 90 million years ago.

Simon Conway Morris, paleobiologist at Cambridge University, notes that this process of convergence is rampant in the evolutionary record, be it at the level of proteins, organisms, or social systems. He argues that, because of convergence, the appearance of sentient beings similar to humans on Earth was inevitable and that extraterrestrial life, should it exist, may not be terribly different from the biological organisms we know from Earth.[34]

The 'Tree' of Life

At the end of the eighteenth century, the Swedish naturalist, Carolus Linnaeus, established the classification system for all life forms that is still applied today. He organized animals and plants into a hierarchy (kingdom, phylum, class, order, family, genus, and species) that is based upon the increasing specificity. Linnaeus based his classification on the shape and anatomy of organisms. The more similar the anatomical structures of creatures looked, the closer they lie within this classification scheme. For two hundred years this classification has worked well and was little changed. In the 1980s, however, cell biologists showed that they could refine this scheme by using the genetic make-up of RNA in organisms. This turned out to be particularly important in the classification of simple, single-celled organisms, many of which look similar.

All organisms biosynthesize proteins in the ribosomes using ribosomal RNA (or rRNA). The order of each base (the A, C, G, T bases mentioned above with regards to DNA) within the rRNA sequence is determined by information encoded within the DNA of the cell. Because similar organisms have similar patterns of rRNA, this is a powerful way to determine how closely organisms are related in the path of evolution. When biochemists applied this classification scheme to the rRNA from all organisms, they found that the tree of life was far more complex than had been established by Linnaeus; indeed, one might better call it a bush or a shrub, rather than a tree.

Biologists have long known that there are two distinct types of single-celled organisms, prokaryotes and eukaryotes.

Prokaryotes are organisms consisting of a very simple cell that is essentially a sac of chemicals containing many proteins, abundant ribosomes and a single loop of DNA. The cells of eukaryotes are more complex. They contain separate compartments, called organelles, where most of the cell's important functions take place. Perhaps the most important of the organelles are the nucleus, which contains the chromosomes of the cell, and the mitochondria, which is the site where most of the energy production of the cell takes place. Because the metabolic functions of the mitochondria require oxygen, most eukaryotes are aerobic.

Based upon variations in rRNA, biologists recently divided prokaryotes into two distinct groups, which they called the *eubacteria* and *archaebacteria*. To accommodate this basic division they added another level to the Linnean classification, which they called *domain*. A domain is a category that stands above *kingdom*. The three domains recognized in their classification are the Eubacteria, Archaea, and Eucarya (Figure 14). A major question in this construction is where does the last common ancestor of all life, which is generally called *last universal common ancestor* (LUCA), lie? Although biologists can use rRNA to construct the tree of life, it is not easy to use the genetic makeup of these organisms to determine where LUCA is because, as we noted above, these simple life forms indulge in wholesale transfer of genetic material. Thus, the genetic makeup of modern single-celled organisms may be very different from similar organisms that existed many millions of years ago. The traditional view is that LUCA lies somewhere in Archaea (Figure 14) or Eubacteria and that Eukarya evolved from these early prokaryotes.

Two important features stand out from this scheme. First is that the plants and animals, which appear to dominate life on our planet, make up only two small branches of the more than 20 major evolutionary limbs on the Tree of Life. The second thing is that the Tree of Life is overwhelmingly made up of microscopic creatures. Of the twenty-three lineages, only three (fungi, plants, and animals) contain individuals that can be seen with the naked eye and each of these also contain microscopic members.

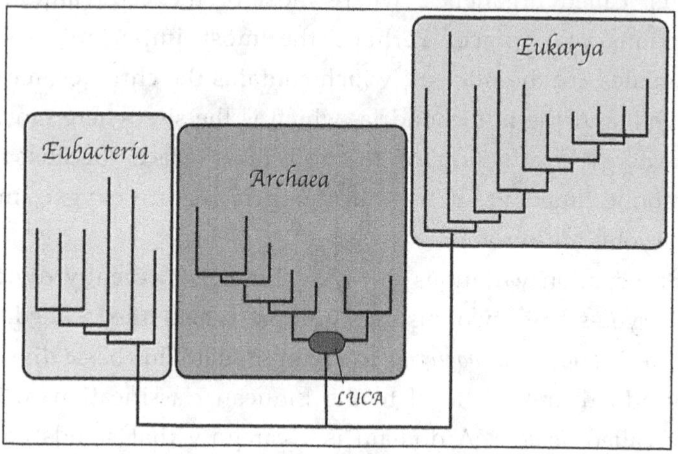

Figure 14 Diagram showing the Tree of Life constructed assuming that the last common universal ancestor (LUCA) was seated in Archaea[35].

Our bias toward creatures that we can see obviously skews our view of evolution. Paleontologists have constructed a detailed history of evolution since the Cambrian, when animals with hard parts appeared in the fossil record. The evolution of land plants, which are easily fossilized, is also fairly well recorded. However, the fossil record only tells an incomplete story of two branches of the Tree of Life. The rest of the history of life, which covers nearly 4000 million years of geologic history, is almost entirely hidden from our view. It has only been in the last decade or so that scientists armed with the techniques of molecular biology have begun to unravel this hidden story.

Chapter 9
The Origin of Life

Even the oldest rocks that have clearly been deposited on the surface of the Earth, which are around 3850 million years old, carry evidence of life. This evidence comes from the isotopic composition of the carbon in these rocks. Carbon occurs in two major isotopes, ^{12}C and ^{13}C. The carbon in the atmosphere has a fixed proportion of ^{12}C and ^{13}C. When organisms make hydrocarbons from atmospheric carbon, they preferentially extract light carbon, and this makes biogenic carbon isotopically distinct from carbon that accumulated by processes unrelated to biologic activity. The carbonaceous material found in the oldest known sedimentary rocks is isotopically light, meaning that it must have been deposited by biologic processes. Thus, by the time that the meteorite bombardment of Earth eased to the point that the rock record could be preserved; life was already present in the oceans.

This is a bit disturbing because it means that we can obtain very little geologic evidence of HOW life appeared on Earth. As geologists sift through the fragments that are preserved of the early Earth, they can infer much about the compositions of the atmosphere and the oceans. They even can estimate the length of the day and how many days there were in a year. However, they cannot say for certain how life formed because it was already present in the oldest rocks we have! What we know about the origin of life comes mainly from inference.

Until a few decades ago, the question of the origin of life seemed to be something that lay well outside of the realm of scientific research. After all, what could science say about something that took place before the geologic record began? Early in the twentieth century a few brave scientists ventured into this field, but it was a lonely endeavor indeed. Then, in the latter portion of the twentieth century, an explosion of discoveries opened important doors to the study of life's origins. First, the lunar program established the age of the moon, and hence allowed us to determine when the Earth differentiated. This gave geochemists the information they needed to calculate the composition of the early atmosphere with some degree of certainty. Second, oceanographic studies discovered widespread vents on the sea floor that teemed with unusual life forms. This alerted scientists to the huge new variety of geochemical environments that life has been able to exploit. Finally, biochemical studies outlined the nature of the Tree of Life and showed how the one-celled organisms, which were originally simply grouped together as 'bacteria,' are differentiated. These advances provided geochemists and biochemists with critical information from which to formulate theories; and against which to test them. Consequently, over the past decades, the study of life's origins has burgeoned into a vital and lively field.

There are three major models for the origin of life (Figure 15). These include:

1) Panspermia: the concept that life was introduced to Earth by a meteorite or comet.
2) The primeval soup theory, which is the idea that life originated in an early ocean that was awash with organic chemicals of abiotic origin.
3) The hydrothermal spring theory, which proposes that life originated at sea floor hydrothermal springs.

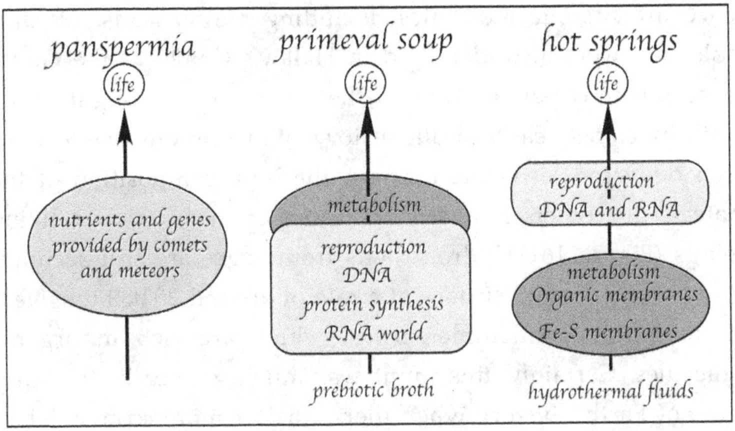

Figure 15 Three models for the origin of life. In *panspermia,* life arrived already developed from space. In the *primeval soup* model, life originated as a self-duplicating molecule in the prebiotic broth. A sophisticated metabolism evolved concurrently or after the evolution of reproduction. In the *hot spring* model, life began around hot springs on the ocean floor. Here metabolism began as reactions within inorganic membranes. These were later replaced by organic membranes, and the genetic codes for reproduction developed within these membranes.

Panspermia

The panspermia theory originated in the late nineteenth century, partially in response to the prevailing model of Lord Kelvin, which indicated that the Earth was only 20 to 40 million years old. If the Earth were that young, there was hardly any time for life to evolve on Earth; thus, the panspermia theory was a convenient way to get life here ready-made. In some ways this theory was prescient, for the formulators could hardly have known that modern radioastronomy would identify a wide variety of organic compounds in interstellar space. The most abundant gas, of course, is H_2 and the abundances of all other compounds are considered in relation to it. Compounds that are present in abundances about 0.001% of hydrogen are CO_2, H_2O, N_2, and H_2CO. The last is formaldehyde, the simplest hydrocarbon. In fact, more than 3/4 of the molecules identified in interstellar space are organic molecules, including amino acids. Organic molecules were also identified in Halley's Comet as the Giotto spacecraft flew past it. Thus, if the oceans were brought to the Earth by comets early in our history, hydrocarbons would have been delivered also. Interestingly, the bulk composition of the material in comets is nearly the same as that found in living beings (Figure 16). Hydrocarbons from space are still accumulating on the Earth's surface at a rate of around 20,000 tons/year in the form of micrometeorites, which are rich in organic molecules. Certainly, this input was much greater in the early years of Earth's history when there was far more cosmic debris hanging around our neighborhood in space. All of this suggests that there may be more than a germ of truth to the panspermia theory.

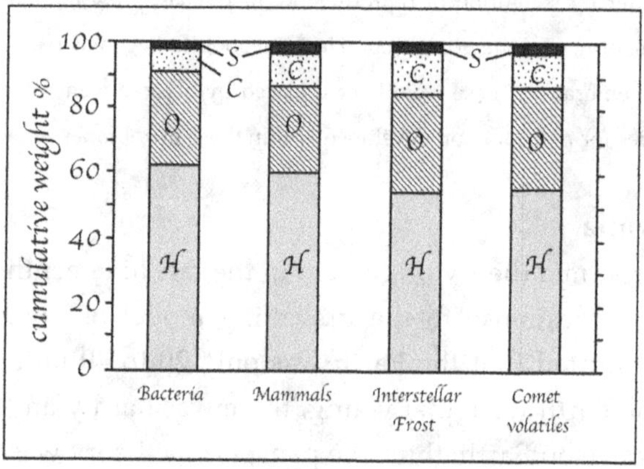

Figure 16 A comparison of the compositions of bacteria, mammals, interstellar frost, and the volatiles in comets[36].

There is little dispute that many of the elements necessary for terrestrial life, and perhaps organic molecules themselves, may have had an extraterrestrial origin. There is considerable doubt, however, about whether these meteors and comets also brought life with them. The main argument against the panspermia theory is that the extraterrestrial amino acids contain an equal proportion of left- and right-handed symmetries. This means that they were almost certainly of abiotic origin, because, as I noted in the previous chapter, organically derived amino acids (at least on Earth) are entirely left-handed. Furthermore, the theory of panspermia doesn't really answer the problem of how life originated; it only pushes it into a different venue.

Primeval Soup Model

Darwin first formulated the Primeval Soup theory in a very general way in a letter to his friend Joseph Hooker in 1871:

> But if (Oh, and what a big if) we could conceive in a warm little pond, with all sorts of ammonia and phosphoric salts, light, heat, electricity, etc., present that a protein compound was chemically formed, ready to undergo still more complex changes, at the present day such matter would be instantly devoured or absorbed, which would never have been the case before living creatures were formed.

The Russian, Alexander Oparin, and the Briton, John Haldane, fleshed the theory out in the 1920s. Oparin and Haldane postulated that in the reducing atmosphere on the early Earth, organic molecules formed by abiotic processes. In their models, the molecules built up in the ocean making 'primeval soup'. As these compounds became more complex, they gave rise to fatty droplets that played the role of protocells within which life eventually evolved.

The Primeval Soup theory was completely untested until 1953 when the University of Chicago graduate student, Stanley Miller, and his adviser, Harold Urey, made a crucial experiment. They built a glass apparatus that consisted of a large upper sphere connected to a lower sphere. The lower sphere contained a model of seawater, while the upper sphere contained a mixture of methane, ammonia, and hydrogen sulfide, which Miller and

Urey thought was similar to the atmosphere of the early Earth. They subjected this atmosphere to a series of electrical charges that were meant to model lightning. After a week of continuous electrical activity the bulb with the model seawater contained a complex mixture of organic molecules, including amino acids.

These experiments were taken to be critical proof that the compounds necessary for life could arise abiotically. Unfortunately, in the late 1980s, geochemists recognized that the Earth's early atmosphere was probably not as reducing as the model atmosphere used by Miller and Urey. Rather than consisting mainly of CH_4, NH_4 and H_2S, the atmosphere was composed of CO_2, N_2, and SO_2. Experiments using this less-reduced atmosphere do not produce the rich mixture of organic molecules found in the Miller and Urey experiments. None the less, recent studies maintain that complex hydrocarbons could have been produced in these CO_2-rich environments by heating, cooling, hydration, or dehydration reactions in tidal regions or by reactions involving radiation in the atmosphere. The yields of organic molecules via these processes would not be as spectacular as those found in Miller and Urey's experiments, but this is not too worrisome considering that the molecules would not break down very fast in the reducing atmosphere and that nature had millions of years with which to work.

Christopher Wills and Jeffrey Bada recently put forth the most elaborate description of the Primordial Soup Theory.[37] They maintain that the prebiotic oceans on Earth were teeming with organic molecules and this wealth of organic molecules would have formed in the tidal zone marginal to the oceans where the primeval soup was subjected to repeated desiccation and hydration and intense ultraviolet radiation. In their model, a thick slime formed by a type of pre-biotic evolution would soon coat the rocks and sand of the tidal flats. This slime would be composed of those molecules that could cling most tightly to the rocks and would grow most readily from the available ingredients in the primordial soup. Wills and Bada contend that the first life would have formed within this slimy laboratory.

In their model, the first step toward life was the development of self-duplicating molecules within the slime. These molecules would be able to produce duplicates of themselves by extracting compounds from the slime. Initially, these may have been simple organic compounds, but eventually they were replaced by naked RNA molecules, which may have been able to duplicate themselves. This stage in the evolution of life has been called 'the RNA world'. Some scientists maintain that the RNA need not have existed as naked molecules in the primordial slime, but was absorbed instead on clays. After some indeterminate amount of time, the RNA became able to synthesize proteins and the proteins took over the catalytic processes of life. Finally, DNA evolved to take the seat of the genetic record, producing virus-like organisms called protobionts. After a genetic code developed, true Darwinian evolution involving competition and natural selection took over, leading to the amazing variety of living organisms that surround us today.

The primeval soup theory concentrates on the ability of molecules to duplicate themselves while the formation of metabolism is considered a secondary process. The self-duplicating process is, of course, a simple form of metabolism, but it does not involve any active input or extraction of energy on behalf of the duplicating molecule. In this model, the protobionts (i.e. early, near-life forms) were heterotrophs; they fed off the primeval soup (or primeval slime), though again the metabolism was very simple. The sophisticated metabolism of autotrophs, both photoautotrophs and chemoautotrophs, evolved later.

The Hot Springs Model

Some geochemists argue that, because the Earth's atmosphere was never highly reducing, the primordial soup never existed. Furthermore, as noted earlier, the early Earth was bathed in withering ultraviolet (UV) radiation, which would have made it difficult or impossible for life to evolve on the Earth's surface, or even in shallow seawater. This has led some scientists to postulate that life originated around vents on the ocean floor, where the deep water protected it from the UV radiation. Scientists advocating the Hot Springs model base their theory on three simple observations. First, because sulfur and transition metals, such as iron, nickel, and cobalt, play important roles in microbial metabolism, it is reasonable to assume that metal sulfides, which are abundant in oceanic vents, played an important role in the origin of life. In particular, the reaction:

$$FeS + H_2S = FeS_2 + H_2 \quad (2)$$

(where FeS = pyrrhotite, and FeS_2 = pyrite) could generate sufficient energy to drive many hydrocarbon-producing reactions.

Second, thermal vents which are common in mid-ocean ridges, are the most geochemically active areas on the Earth's surface. New oceanic crust is continually being generated at these ridges and heat from this active volcanism drives huge hydrothermal circulation systems that are responsible for the vents. During the early years of Earth history, when volcanism was more intense, these hydrothermal systems would have been much more extensive than they are today. Third, the chemical gradients between the fluids in the vents and the ocean water is more than adequate to provide all the energy needed to drive the construction of the complex organic molecules necessary for life.

According to the major advocates for this model, Michael Russell and Alan Hall[38], reaction of a sulfur-rich hydrothermal fluid with the iron-rich seawater of early Earth would have precipitated hollow globules of amorphous Fe-sulfide. These globules would be similar to the 0.1 to 1.0 mm (.004 - .04 in) diameter sulfide-coated bubbles that have been produced in the laboratory and to the imprints of structures reported from ancient ocean-floor vents. The Fe-sulfide coating could serve as a semi-permeable membrane between the reducing vent fluid and the relatively oxidizing seawater. It was within this coated globule that the reactions necessary for life took place.

This model maintains that carbon dioxide and nitrogen would be concentrated against the membrane in areas of low fluid flow, where they would be hydrogenated to form the hydrocarbons and ammonia molecules necessary for life. These organic molecules would adhere to the sulfide membrane and become increasingly complex as reactions proceeded. Eventually, the complex hydrocarbons would take the place of sulfide membranes as the container for life. As the organic molecules within the protocell became more complex, RNA and DNA evolved, making processes of reproduction typical of organisms possible.

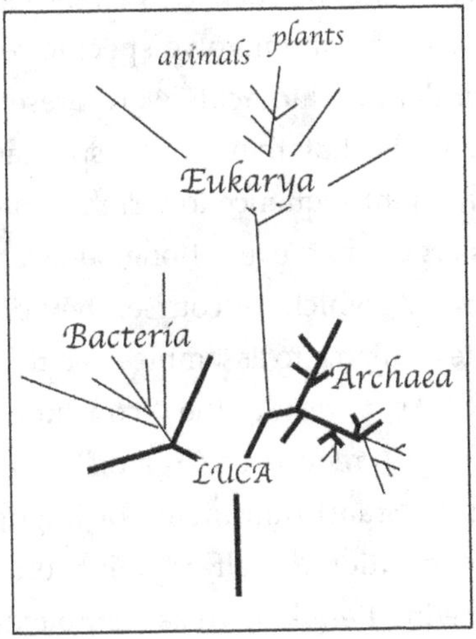

Figure 17 The tree of life constructed assuming LUCA roots in hyperthermophile prokaryotes (heavy lines)[39].

The hot spring model differs in many respects from the primeval soup model, not least of all in the fact that in this model metabolism came first, followed later by reproduction (Figure 15). The advocates of the hot spring model maintain that the last universal common ancestor (LUCA) lies among hyperthermophile prokaryotes (Figure 17). These are bacteria that are most at home at extreme temperatures (80° to 113°C or 176° to 235°F). They may survive at lower temperatures, and many are found in samples of common seawater, but they only reproduce at extreme temperatures. Most of these bacteria are anerobic. Those scientists who back the primeval soup theory contend that this is not a compelling argument because, as noted in the previous chapter, there is a huge debate as to where in the Tree of Life LUCA lies. Furthermore, even if LUCA was a hyperthermophile, it doesn't necessarily support the hot springs model because, as noted above, the primeval oceans themselves may have been hot.

Self-Organization

Creationists and advocates of Intelligent Design argue that, because the proteins necessary for life involve specific sequences of amino acids, even if abundant amino acids were present in a primordial environment, the odds that they could spontaneously assemble themselves into the right sequence to form a protein is exceedingly slim. Creationists argue that, even if one believed that the Earth is 4500 million years old (which, of course, they don't), there would not be enough time available to assemble even the simplest proteins necessary for life. As a result, they conclude that simply the presence of life on Earth requires a Creator.

This is not so says Stuart Kauffman, for it ignores the powerful process of 'self-organization'.[40] Self-organization is a process that is studied by the growing field known as Complexity Theory. Unlike reductionist science, which studies the balance of energy in closed systems, Complexity Theory is a holistic field of science that deals with the dissipation of energy in open systems. Under appropriate situations some open systems will spontaneously form structures that are stable over a range of conditions. This phenomenon is called self-organization. A good example of self-organization is the way that a whirlpool will spontaneously appear as water drains from your bathtub. Self-organization may also happen in chemical systems by the process known as autocatalysis.

To understand how autocatalysis proceeds, let us assume that there is a primordial soup composed of various amino acids. These amino acids could string together to make complex proteins by reactions such as:

$$A + B = \gamma \ (3)$$
$$X + Y = \zeta \ (4)$$

A, B, X, and Y stand for amino acids or groups of amino acids and γ and ζ represent complex proteins. As Creationists point out, the production of proteins requires stringing amino acids together in exactly the correct sequence. On their own, reactions (3) and (4) are not likely to be very efficient. As a result, one would expect that our primordial soup would consist mainly of amino acids with vanishingly small amounts of γ and ζ.

Things would be very different if protein ζ acts as a template that makes it easier for A and B to combine to make γ and if protein γ acts as a template that makes it easier for X and Y to react to ζ. Such a template is called a 'catalyst'. A catalyst is a compound that speeds up a reaction but is neither consumed nor produced by the reaction. To symbolize the catalyzed reactions we can write them as:

$$A + B + \zeta = \gamma + \zeta \ (5)$$
$$X + Y + \gamma = \zeta + \gamma \ (6)$$

Initially, there would be very little of either γ or ζ available to catalyze the reactions. However, once even a single molecule of γ has been produced by reaction (3), it becomes available to catalyze reaction (6). The molecule of ζ produced by reaction (6) then becomes available to catalyze reaction (5), which produces more γ, which can further catalyze reaction (6). This feedback process, called autocatalysis, is shown schematically by arrows in Figure (18).

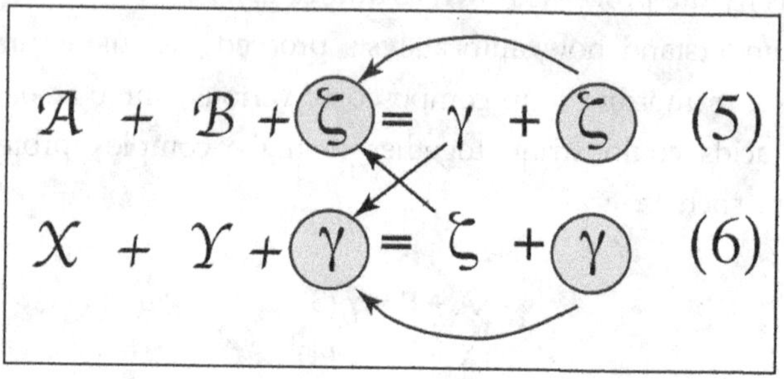

Figure 18 Diagram showing an example of autocatalysis. Reactions (5) and (6) may be too sluggish to produce even small amounts compounds γ and ζ. However, if γcatalyzes reaction (5) and ζ catalyses reaction (6), then the feedback between the two reactions can produce large amounts of γ and ζ.

Kaufmann argues that, because many organic compounds are both products of reactions and catalysts to other reactions, any mix of amino acids are likely to undergo self-organization by autocatalysis. In addition, there is a growing field of data indicating that many common minerals may also catalyze the production of organic compounds. A particularly good example of this is clay, which is a common alteration product found in ocean floor vents. Clays are minerals that are composed of exceedingly tiny sheets of silica combined with aluminum, magnesium, or iron. Between these layers, clays can absorb large amounts water, which is what makes clay slippery. Mineralogists have recently discovered that organic molecules will be concentrated between the layers of clays, making clays a possible breeding area for life. Thus, because of the phenomenon of self-organization, the production of complex organic compounds by inorganic reactions may not be as hopelessly unlikely as Creationists would like us to believe.

This self-organization process could have taken place in the manner suggested by either the primordial soup or the hot-spring model. It could have taken place in a globule of organic molecules clinging to a rock, within the interlayers of clay, or in inclusions of iron sulfides. Wherever it took place, the concept self-organization adds a new dimension to both these models. Whereas the original models would predict that either reproduction or metabolism evolved first, with self-organization, both respiration and reproduction could have arisen at the same time.

Summary

Research on the origin of life is making it increasingly clear that there is little difference between abiotic geochemical processes on the Earth's surface and the metabolism of simple organisms. Thus, the once yawning gap between life and non-living matter, which used to require Divine intervention to bridge, is becoming narrower and narrower. Despite the great progress that has been made in this field over the past decades, however, it is safe to say that we may never know exactly how the first life developed on this planet. The geologic record of this great event is non-existent, so all of our evidence is circumstantial. This explains why very different models have been constructed from the same data.

Although scientists have made significant progress in the past decades toward understanding life's origins, they still have to overcome one major problem. All the models that have been presented so far suffer from the same critical flaw; they are exceedingly vague in explaining *how* DNA and RNA, the vital building blocks of life actually developed. Until someone comes up with a valid reaction path that can model the formation of DNA and RNA by abiotic processes with thermodynamic rigor, models for the origin of life will remain slightly above the level of scientific speculation.

Chapter 10
The History of Life

Fossil Evidence for Evolution

Before I discuss the history of life on Earth I must address whether the geologic record faithfully records this history. One of the key arguments of Creationists is that the fossil record is full of holes. They argue that Darwinism cannot work because species appear suddenly in the fossil record with no intermediate steps.[41] Unfortunately, the folks who make this statement either don't understand the nature of the fossil record or choose to obfuscate it.

To understand the problems of interpreting life history from the geologic record, let's do a little mental experiment. Let's assume that you have encountered a junkyard that faithfully records the history of the automobile in first half of the 20th century. Let's also assume that every car produced in the United States has a one-in-a-million chance of ending up in that junkyard. In the dump, the junked cars are interlayered with copies of the *New York Times* giving the year it was junked. Your friend, a well-trained automobile-paleontologist could identify the make and design of the car from pieces of fender or a drive shaft and thus, despite the time lag of a few years between the construction of cars and their demise in the junkyard, he or she can construct a fairly good history of the evolution of automobiles.

After a careful study of the remains of autos in the junkyard your friend concludes that sometime between 1915 and 1917 the model T Ford appeared suddenly with no intermediate steps between it and a horse-drawn buggy. This sudden appearance completely belies the written history of the automobile, which tells us that the very earliest autos, which looked like buggies with motors attached, appeared in the earliest years of the 18th century and that mass production of autos began in the mid-1880s. Unfortunately, only a very limited number of the earliest cars were produced. Production increased substantially around 1910 (Figure 19), but only by 1917 were more than a million cars produced per year. Because the junkyard had only a one-in-a-million chance of sampling the cars that were being produced, only by 1915 or so would there be a very good chance of cars appearing in the junkyard. Because of this, it is understandable that the first car you would find in your junkyard, resting upon a variety of horse-drawn buggies would be the relatively advanced Model T. There would be virtually no chance that your junkyard recorded either the earliest autos or the rapid evolution that autos made during the latter years of the 19th Century.

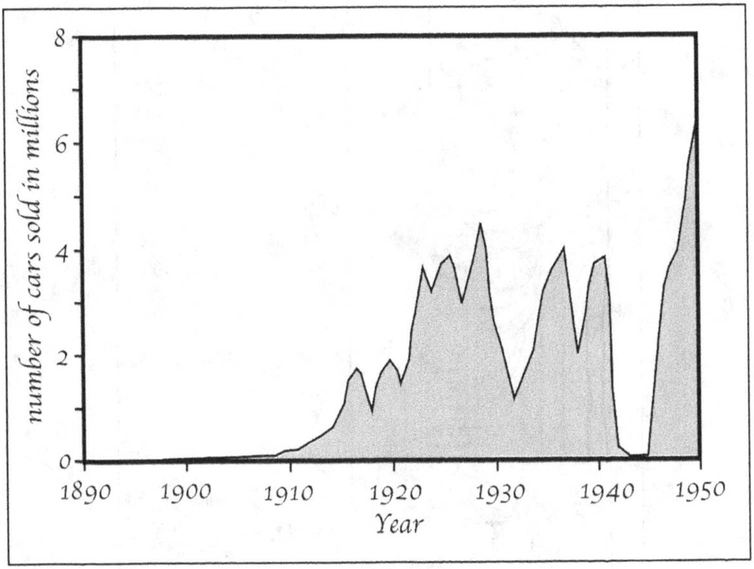

Figure 19 Cars Sold in the US from 1900 until 1950[42].

This little story is very much like what one finds in the fossil record. It is very rare for a dead animal to become fossilized. As any rancher could tell you, the body of a steer that has died on the range is quickly consumed; within a few months nothing remains but a few widely scattered bones. To become a fossil, a dead creature must be buried in sediment shortly after death and that sediment cannot be subjected to erosion before a geologist comes along to discover it. Because it is so difficult for an animal to be fossilized, a given species must attain a substantial population before any member of it is likely to appear in the fossil record. When a new species appears on Earth, it consists of only a few individuals and the genetic make up of these individuals may change considerably as the species adjusts itself to its new niche. By the time this species has developed a large enough population to make a contribution to the fossil record, it may look significantly different from the species from which it arose.

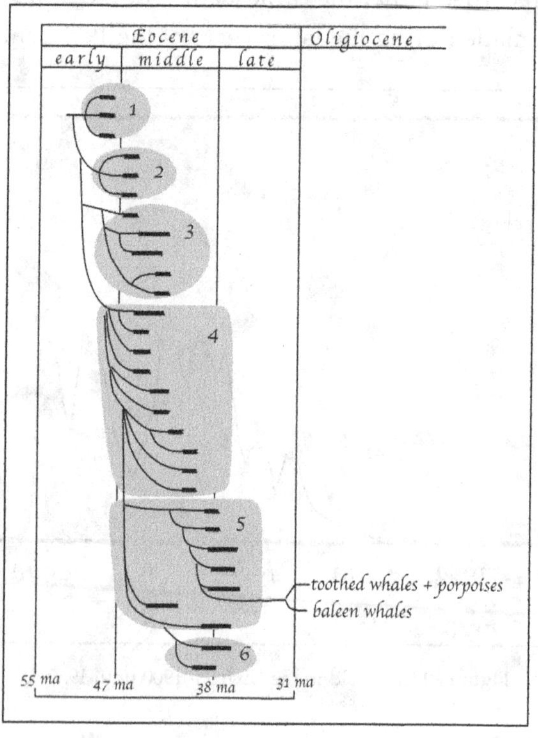

Figure 20 Time line for the evolution of the order Cetacea. Shaded areas give the six families recognized in the fossil record. Heavy lines represent different genera in the families[43].

Despite the inherent uncertainty of the fossil record, and contrary to the arguments of the Creationists, the story of evolution recorded in the rocks is amazingly complete. For example, paleontologists can reconstruct from the fossil record the evolution of horses, elephants, whales, and humans in great detail. As an example, I have chosen the evolution of whales because modern whales (and their relatives, dolphins and porpoises) look very different from any likely precursor. At the time he wrote the *Origin of the Species*, Darwin was clearly uncertain about how they arose; he felt that perhaps they descended from bears. It has only been the past few decades that rich fossil deposits in south Asia have allowed paleontologists to construct a detailed family tree for whales and their relatives.

All the action in the evolution of whales took place in the Eocene epoch, between 50 and 35 million years ago. Paleontologists recognize seven families in the order Cetacea (the order to which whales, dolphins, and porpoises belong) that arose during this time (Figure 20). To save the reader the agony of dealing with the long Latin names for these families, I simply refer to them in Figure 20 by the numbers 1 through 7. The basal family for whale evolution consisted of long-legged, dog-sized animals that are only known from the Eocene sediments of Pakistan and India. Apart from whales, the closest modern relative to this family are pigs and deer. Because of their long legs they were probably poor swimmers and paleontologists believe that they lived on land. Fossils from families two and three are also restricted to southern Asia. Animals in these families had shorter legs that those of family 1 and were clearly good swimmers. Members of family 2 probably spent part of their time on land; those from family 3 were almost entirely aquatic.[44] Fossils of family four are found from around the world, indicating that this family is the first of the early whales to live in the open ocean. These animals probably looked a lot like modern seals with flippers and a streamlined body. Family 5 was a complex and diverse family that probably looked very similar to modern dolphins, with a streamlined body, fluked tail, and small back legs that were probably little use in swimming. The modern families of whales, dolphins, and porpoises arose from this family around 38 million years ago.

During the evolution from family 1 to family 5, the nose holes of these animals moved from the end of the snout, where they are in most terrestrial animals, to the top of the head, where they are in whales. The body became streamlined and a huge fluked tail appeared, while the joints in the extremities fused into flippers. These anatomical differences, along with many other more subtle ones, make sense only in the context of progressive adaptation to an aquatic environment; an adaptation that took place over about fifteen million years.[45]

We have a very good record of the evolution of whales and other mammals because it happened relatively recently, which means that we have a large number of sedimentary sequences of that age from which to construct this history. It is a little more difficult to construct the evolution of dinosaurs and even more difficult to read the history of fishes or the earliest land vertebrates because the further back in Earth history one goes, the fewer fossil-bearing beds from a given age are preserved. Nonetheless, the history I relate below is well constrained and is consistent with all the geologic and paleontological information we have to date.

The Earth 600 Million Years Ago

If you had visited the Earth 600 million years ago, you would have found the planet to be slightly improved from the hellish place you visited 3400 million years earlier. You would not have needed the heavy spacesuit that was necessary on the previous visit, for, by now, the temperature had become more moderate and there was enough ozone in the atmosphere to block the ultraviolet light from space. However, you might still need oxygen tanks to survive because there may not have been enough oxygen to support humans (or any other animal). The atmosphere would have cleared up significantly since your last visit, but even so, it probably would still be hazy because there were no surface plants around to hold down the dust.

You would still find the Earth's surface to be barren but, unlike your last visit, it would be graced by touches of color. The exposed rocks and soil would have a distinct brownish or reddish tinge, for now there was enough oxygen in the atmosphere to oxidize the iron. You might even find a hint of green in the damper areas where algal mats had taken hold. Colorful slimy algal mats also lined the tidal flats and shallow waters of rivers and lakes, but it would have been difficult to find life any more advanced than that. Considering that algae was a pretty anemic achievement to show after such a long period of evolution, you may have assumed that life on this planet would never amount to much.

Little would you have known that you were severely underestimating the changes that had taken place since your last visit. The effects of biological and chemical evolution on the Earth over the previous 3400 million years had been profound. The reddish rocks on the surface of the Earth and the presence of the ozone shield were by products of biological evolution. Before complex oxygen-loving organisms like us could gambol around on this planet, biological processes had to change the chemistry of the atmosphere, oceans, and the surface of the planet, and this was a slow process. By 600 million years ago, all the hard work had been done, and life on Earth was poised to explode into a myriad of forms that would eventually lead to humans (Figure 21).

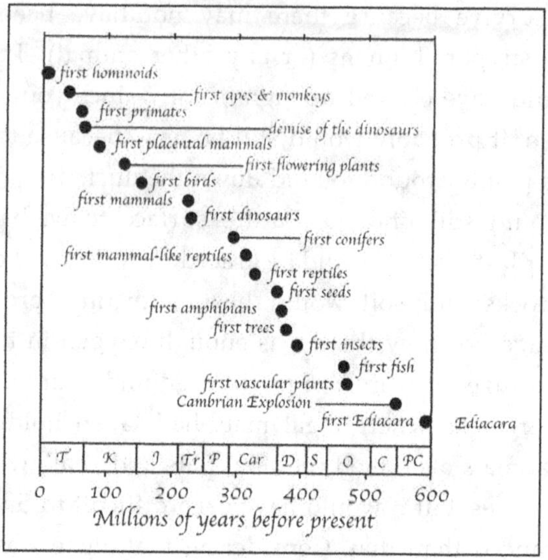

Figure 21 Landmarks on the evolution of life during the past 600 million years. PC = Precambrian, C = Cambrian, O = Ordovician, S = Silurian, D = Devonian, Car = Carboniferous, P = Permian, Tr = Triassic, J = Jurassic, K = Cretaceous, T = Tertiary.

Evolution of the Atmosphere

Regardless of how it got here, as soon as life arrived, its metabolism began changing the planet. The first effect was to alter the composition of the Earth's atmosphere, which, after time, altered the composition of the crust as well. As we noted in Chapter 7, the atmosphere on our planet initially was dominated by N_2, H_2O, and CO_2 and had only tiny amounts of free oxygen. In Chapter 8 we noted that the basic reaction for biologic metabolism consumes CO_2 plus water and produces carbohydrates plus free oxygen. Nominally, this reaction should have no effect on the atmosphere, because when the single-celled critters in the early seas died, the reaction would run in reverse and oxygen would be consumed during the decay of the protoplasm. In reality, however, a certain proportion of the organic matter formed on the sea floor became incorporated into the sediment, where it was unavailable for oxidation. The oxygen that was produced during the formation of this organic material would therefore be free to do geologic work.

Initially, the oxygen released by this process was consumed by oxidizing iron from Fe^{2+} to Fe^{3+}. Thus, as long as there was any ferrous iron available on the Earth's surface for oxidation, the oxygen content of the atmosphere remained very low. The Earth's crust contains a lot of iron and it took nearly two thousand million years for the oxygen produced by metabolism to oxidize all of the exposed iron. Finally, around 2300 million years ago, the last of the ferrous iron available in the exposed rocks was oxidized. After this point the oxygen pressure began to build up in the atmosphere (Figure 22). We know that the oxygen pressure in the atmosphere exceeded about 0.03 bars by about 2100 million years ago, because this is the time when sandstones that are stained red by oxidized iron became common in the geologic record.

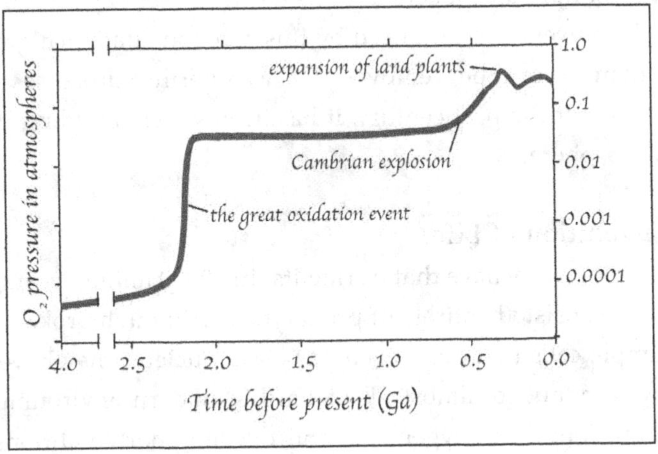

Figure 22 The change in the oxygen content of the atmosphere over Earth's history[46]. Ga = giga annum (1000s of millions of years).

We have very few constraints on the path followed by the oxygen pressure of the atmosphere between 2100 million years ago and around 300 million years, mainly because there are few chemical equilibria available within sediments that one could use to monitor it[47]. Carbon and sulfur isotopic abundances in sedimentary rocks suggest oxygen reached a peak at a pressure of around 0.35 bars about 300 million years ago and attained another smaller peak around 100 million years ago (Fig. 22). As we will see, these changes in atmospheric composition had a profound effect on the evolution of life.

Interestingly, the reaction modeling metabolism (reaction (1)) is precisely the reaction that is responsible for the increase in atmospheric CO_2 that has accompanied the industrial age. In this instance the hydrocarbons (as modeled by H_2CO) represent the organic fuels that have been extracted from the Earth in the form of petroleum or coal. The burning of these hydrocarbons consumes O_2 and produces H_2O and CO_2. The O_2 required for this reaction is continually replenished into the atmosphere by the metabolism of plants, and the H_2O produced from this reaction simply disappears into the Earth's water budget. Carbon dioxide, however, is produced by this reaction at a much greater rate than it can be removed by weathering processes and therefore, for the past century, it has been slowly building up in the atmosphere.

The Evolution of Life

Paleontologists believe that during its first 2000 million years, life on Earth consisted entirely of prokaryotes. Although prokaryotes are simple cells that don't even possess a nucleus, they have the ability to adapt to almost all of Earth's modern environments. They are found in oxygen-rich and oxygen-poor conditions, at temperatures from near freezing to boiling, and in waters that range from alkalic to very acidic. Prokaryotes have no mechanism for independent movement and reproduce by simple cloning, which means that one cell subdivides to make an exact duplicate of itself. One would not expect this process to be particularly prone to the formation of mutations, but mutation was probably not the only pathway followed by evolution in single-celled animals. It turns out the single-celled animals (both prokaryotes and eukaryotes) are shamelessly promiscuous and are able to exchange genes readily with other single-celled creatures. Thus, it is likely that evolution in early life proceeded not so much by mutation but by reticulate evolution, which is what this exchange of genes has been called.

Development of Eukaryotes

Perhaps the most important breakthrough during evolution was the formation of eukaryotes, because all higher animals and plants belong to this domain. Most eukaryotes are aerobic, so they are not likely to have evolved before free oxygen appeared in the atmosphere. Our poorly constrained knowledge of Precambrian paleontology indicates that eukaryotes appeared on the scene 2100 million years ago, which is shortly after the oxygen content of the atmosphere began to increase. This timing is critical, because complex organisms couldn't evolve until oxygen contents rose to about 3% of the present atmospheric levels. Only at this level is there sufficient oxygen to produce enough ozone to protect the surface of the Earth and the shallower portions of the sea from the lethal effects of ultraviolet radiation.

As I noted in Chapter 8, the key difference between eukaryotes and prokaryotes is that the former contain organelles. These organelles are host to the genes and mitochondria, which is where most of the metabolism takes place, and for plants, chloroplasts, where we find the seat of photosynthesis. Another difference is that simple eukaryotes have a flagellum, a tail-like appendage that allows the cells to move independently through the water. The DNA in the mitochondria and chloroplasts does not participate in reproduction of eukaryotes, which means that these organelles behave like independent cells within the eukaryote cell.

For this reason, Lynn Margulis postulated that organelles arose as independent prokaryote cells that were enclosed into another prokaryote cell[48]. This process could have happened in ways similar to the promiscuous exchange of genes that single-celled organisms are so adept at. A similar process is seen to take place within the single celled eukaryote, *Paramecium. Paramecium* may contain hundreds of algae, which live happily within the cell, producing nutrients for both themselves and the host cell via photosynthesis. *Paramecium* cells that are raised in the dark will lose their algae guests, but they will pick them up again if introduced to a light-bearing environment where the algae are present. This is called a mutualistic symbiotic relationship, which is an association where two or more creatures grow together for mutual benefit.

The model for the formation of eukaryotes is shown in Figure 23. Incorporation of an aerobic bacterium into an original prokaryote could have produced a mitochondrion (2 in Figure 23). Incorporation of spirochete, common elongate spiral bacteria, on to the margin of the cell could form the flagellum (3 in Figure 23). Plants could have formed by incorporation of cyanobacterium, which can photosynthesize, to form a chloroplast (4 in Figure 23). Because plants have both chloroplasts and mitochondria and animals lack chloroplasts, this model postulates that plants evolved after animals. It is not clear in this model how the nucleus, which is the main characteristic of eukaryotes, formed, nor whether it formed before or after the incorporation of the mitochondria and chloroplasts.

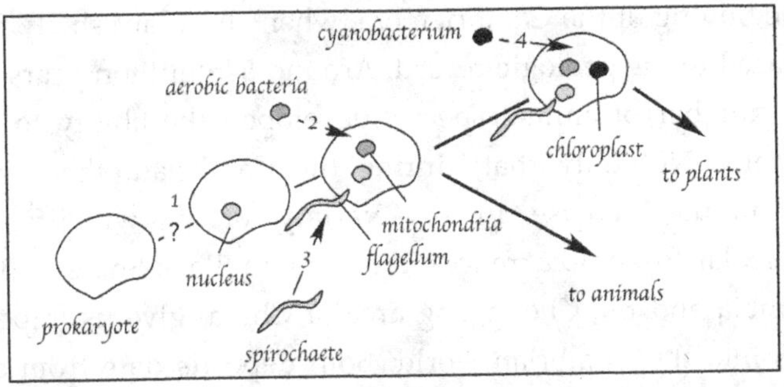

Figure 23 The postulated origin of eukaryotes. 1. The nucleus evolves in some unspecified way. 2. Incorporation of aerobic bacteria could produce mitochondria. 3. Incorporation of spirochete to form a flagellum, 4. Incorporation of cyanobacteria could produce chloroplasts and leads eventually to plants.

The Ediacara

Although the earliest likely eukaryote fossil, carbon films that form curving spirals 1 mm (0.04 in) wide and up to 90 mm (3.5 inches) long, occur in rocks that are 2100 million years old, the first complex community of organisms consisting of more than one cell didn't appear until ca 595 million years ago. This fossil assemblage, which is called the Ediacaran fauna, was made up of bag-shaped creatures some of which may have extended more than a meter (3 feet) in the largest direction. They are preserved in sandstone as round or oblate impressions that locally show some evidence of segmentation or tentacles. There are very few fossil tracks in Ediacaran horizons, suggesting that the creatures must have had a sedentary lifestyle. This indicates that the Ediacaran fauna were either autotrophs or filter feeders. We do not know what kind of creatures made these fossils. They could have been some kind of simple colony of animals or they may have been part of a kingdom of organisms that has long since gone extinct.

The Cambrian Explosion

Perhaps the most striking 'event' in the history of life occurred at the beginning of the Cambrian era, when abundant shelly fossils appeared in the geologic record. Around 545 million years ago a large number of animal species developed the ability to make skeletons. Not only that; during the Cambrian, there was a tremendous increase in the variety of known life. Two spectacular fossil occurrences, the Burgess Black Shale of British Columbia and the Chengjiang area of China, give us important views into the Cambrian world. Both deposits date from about 515 to 520 million years ago with the Burgess Black Shale being somewhat younger than the Chengjiang deposit. These occurrences are special because they contain thousands of fossils in which carbon films in the rocks preserve the shapes of the soft tissues. Many of the fossils are unlike any members of a phylum living today. This means that the diversity of life in the Cambrian period was far greater than we would recognize if we studied only the life forms that produced skeletal remains.

These discoveries indicate that as many as 100 phyla may have existed during the Cambrian, and no more than five of these phyla show any evidence of a Precambrian ancestry. This momentous eruption of life has been called the Cambrian Explosion, and it involved BOTH the development of skeletons and an explosion of life forms, many of which were poorly suited for fossilization.

Many theories have been proposed to explain the Cambrian explosion, but it still remains one of the greatest mysteries in geology and paleontology. The inability of paleontologists to explain the Cambrian Explosion is often used as an argument against Darwinism. Anti-Darwinists maintain that the sudden appearance of such a huge variety of life indicates that some process *other than* natural selection must have been involved. In addition, many Creationist authors, such as Phil Johnson, the author of *Darwin on Trial*[49], contend that the fact that scientists gloss over this great problem proves that science is driven by an atheistic ideology that is not particularly concerned with truth.

The arguments of Johnson and others of the Creationist and Intelligent Design movements unfortunately grossly oversimplify the problem. It is true that the Cambrian Explosion occurred over a geologically short period of time, but it hardly happened instantaneously. Detailed studies show that the Cambrian Explosion involved a gradual increase of faunal diversity over a period of more than 50 million years, stretching from the latest Precambrian into the Middle Cambrian. Furthermore, a growing number of skeletonized invertebrate fossils have been found to overlap with the Ediacaran fossils in the latest Precambrian. Thus, evidence shows that, rather than appearing suddenly and miraculously as the anti-Darwinists maintain, the complex life forms seen in the Chengjiang and Burgess deposits developed over a period of at least 50 million years.

Not only is the 'sudden' appearance of complex life greatly overstated by the Intelligent Design folks; their statement that science cannot explain the Cambrian Explosion is also a great exaggeration. Perhaps the most compelling scientific explanation for the Cambrian Explosion is that it was related to the increase in oxygen in the Earth's oceans.[50]

One theory is that biological organisms couldn't produce collagen until oxygen became high enough in the atmosphere. Collagen is a protein that is necessary for the construction of connective tissues. Such tissues are important both for the development of muscles and for the tissue that connects muscles to bones, exoskeletons and shells. Because the production of collagen is oxygen-intensive, Ken Towe maintains that creatures with skeletons could not have evolved until oxygen pressure had climbed to levels high enough to allow production of collagen[51].

Several authors argue that the oxygen in the atmosphere may have been high enough for living creatures to form collagen well before the Cambrian, but the ocean floor remained anoxic until the very end of the Proterozoic. Because higher animals need oxygen to exist, they could not have evolved until the sea floor became oxygenated. Chemical and isotopic studies show that Proterozoic sediments were deposited in oxygen-poor environments whereas, after the Cambrian, most ocean floor sediments are oxygen-rich. This idea goes something like this: Throughout the later Proterozoic, the upper waters in the ocean were oxygenated and hosted a healthy population of microorganisms, mostly algae. As these algae died, they produced a soup of organic matter that slowly sank to the ocean floor. Decay of this organic soup depleted oxygen from deep ocean waters and kept the ocean floor anoxic. Late in the Precambrian Ediacaran fauna and sponges appeared. These creatures made a living by filtering the organic material out of the water. Over time, as the amount of dead algae settling down on the ocean floor decreased, the oxygen levels on the seafloor increased.

Regardless of whether it reflected an inherent increase in atmospheric oxygen or it happened because primitive organisms such as sponges and Ediacara had consumed the organic soup in the oceans, by the dawn of the Cambrian, for the first time in geologic history, the ocean floor became oxygenated. As the oxygen level on the sea floor increased, large multi-celled organisms evolved. When these organisms developed the ability to produce collagen, lifestyles associated with active muscles became possible. Not only that, the production of collagen meant that animal tissue could adhere to solid material, such as shells. This is the reason why shelly fossils, as well as evidence of active lifestyle such as burrowing and predation, appeared at approximately the same time. The introduction of predation brought about an arms race, in which predators and prey were forced to develop competing strategies to stay alive.

It should not be surprising that the variety of life exploded as creatures took advantage of new means of locomotion, a diversity of new ways of making a living, and competed in a vicious arms race. The explosion was also made possible because the genetic make up of life at the very beginning of the Cambrian was relatively simple. Only small alterations in the genome were necessary to change a worm-like progenitor to fish into a worm-like progenitor to molluscs.

The Evolution of Fish

When the dust of the Cambrian explosion settled, one finds an aquatic world populated with a bewildering array of life forms that crawled upon the seafloor, burrowed into the sediments, or just sat there encased in shells. One of the creatures populating the Chengjiang site in the Early Cambrian was a tiny (up to 4 cm (1.5 in.) long) eel-like creature. Because the fossils from this locality preserve soft tissues, we know that this creature contained tiny eyes, olfactory sacs, and a rudimentary spinal cord running along the dorsal length of its body. This was the first vertebrate and, as such, it was a distant relative of fishes, amphibians, reptiles, birds, and us.

The steps through which these early fish-like creatures evolved to become fishes are still poorly known. The skeletons of these early vertebrates were composed of cartilage, which doesn't fossilize well. As a result, about a 50 million year hiatus lies between the Chengjiang fossil and the first well-preserved fish fossil, which dates from the Ordovician (~ 470 million years ago). This creature contained an internal skeleton as well as ossified armor that covered the head. Unlike modern fishes, the early fish didn't have jaws and looked vaguely like modern-day lampreys. The first known jawed fish appeared in the early Silurian (~ 420 million years ago). The development of jaws and a strong skeleton provided a great evolutionary advantage to fish. The jaws made fish effective killing machines. The bony skeleton provided a solid support for the attachment of muscles and gave greater efficiency for the use of a muscular tail for swimming. As a result, fish soon became the largest predator in the Paleozoic oceans. By the middle of the Devonian (~ 380 million years ago), Piscean predators measuring up to six meters (20 feet) long were patrolling the seas.

The Development of Land Plants

While chordates in the sea were developing from wormy swimming things into giant fish, a great change was sweeping across the terrestrial landscape as plants began colonizing the land. Algal mats may have covered parts of the Earth's surface as early as 2000 to 2200 million years ago, which was shortly after the ozone layer had developed in the atmosphere. However, the oldest clear fossil terrestrial algal mat is about 1000 million years old. The terrestrial plants in the Cambrian were probably not much more advanced than these early mats.

Spore-like microfossils suggest that the first vascular plants had evolved by the mid-Ordovician (~470 million years ago), but the earliest body fossil of a vascular plant, a type of club moss, comes from late Silurian, about 400 million years ago. These early plants had roots and stems for transport of water but their hydraulic systems were not very efficient. As a result, they probably formed communities in areas near water bodies. The increase in abundance and size of root casts within fossil soils indicates that throughout the Silurian and Devonian these plant communities became denser and spread into well-drained uplands. The first trees appear in the geologic record in late Devonian (~ 380 million years ago). These trees had large woody trunks similar to modern trees but they had fern-like leaves and were more closely related to ferns than to conifers or flowering plants. Conifers similar to modern forms appeared in the mid-Carboniferous (~320 million years ago), and they remained the major plant group for the next 200 million years. The final wave in plant evolution occurred in the early Cretaceous when flowering plants (including grasses) appeared and radiated throughout the world. By the end of the Cretaceous (65 million years ago) they had become the major group of land plants.

The colonization of the terrestrial surface by plants in the Carboniferous had great effects on the composition of the Earth's atmosphere. The abundant herbaceous growth extracted vast amounts of CO_2 from the atmosphere, sequestering it in plants. Much of this ended up being taken out of circulation when the plant matter was deposited as peat and coal. This had two effects on the composition of the atmosphere. First, it led to a great decrease in atmospheric CO_2 (Figure 24), which would have cooled the climate, and may have contributed to an ice age in the late Paleozoic. Second, the sequestering of carbon into abundant organic matter would have released vast amounts of oxygen into the atmosphere. Oxygen levels of the atmosphere increased up to perhaps 35% (about 1/3 more than we have today).

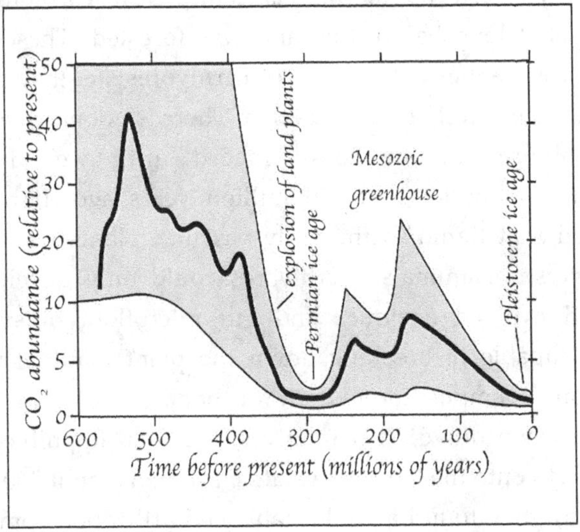

Figure 24 The calculated changes in CO_2 abundance in the atmosphere over time. Shaded area gives the uncertainty in the value[52].

This high oxygen level may have allowed the Carboniferous insects to grow to prodigious sizes. Rather than using the circulation of blood to provide oxygen to their tissues, insects rely on fine tubes called tracheoles. Such a process works well only on a small scale, so circulation of oxygen via tracheoles is a major limiting factor for the size of insects. With the ambient oxygen content of the atmosphere higher in Carboniferous, insects could grow to correspondingly bigger sizes. For example, some dragonflies in the Carboniferous had wingspans that measured up to two feet (60 cm).

Colonization of the Land by Animals

The first evidence for terrestrial animals are tracks of a eurypterid species. These scorpion-like beasts, which may have been as much as a meter (3 feet) long, come ashore in the late Silurian (about 420 million years ago). These fossils are part of the growing evidence that terrestrial environments hosted a vibrant community of arthropods (insects, centipedes, scorpions, mites, spiders, etc.) long before the land was forested. These earliest animals were either detritivores or carnivores; i.e. they lived off the plant debris and off of each other. There is not much evidence for herbivores in the fossil record until well into the Carboniferous period, ca. 330 million years ago. It has been suggested that lignin in the early vascular plants was toxic to early terrestrial animals. Herbivores could only develop after they had evolved enzymes and gut microflora of symbiotic bacteria capable of breaking down the plant material without relying on decomposition to do it for them.

Thus, when our distant relatives, the first amphibious fish, made forays onto the land in the late Devonian (about 360 million years ago), they found a well-established arthropod community on which to dine. These first tetrapods, as these four-legged beasts are called, appear really ungainly to us, for they walked with their fingers (some beasts had six, seven or eight fingers or toes, rather than the five that most beings have today) splayed out to their sides, rather than pointed forward. As the amphibians evolved through the Carboniferous they lost these extra digits and the fingers rotated forward. Amphibians were widespread throughout the Carboniferous, but by the early Permian (~ 280 million years ago) they were slowly replaced by reptiles and mammal-like reptiles.

Appearance of the First Reptiles and Mammals

Geologically speaking, the major varieties of the land vertebrates (amphibians, reptiles, and mammals) all appeared at nearly the same time. Reptiles and mammal-like reptiles arose near the middle of the Carboniferous (338 million years ago), only a few million years after the appearance of amphibians. The mammal-like reptiles and the true reptiles lived side by side throughout the Permian. During this time the mammal-like reptiles, which were the major predators in the Permian, slowly became more mammal-like, making it difficult to mark a time in the geologic record when true mammals appeared. Dinosaurs evolved from the true reptiles in the mid-Triassic (225 million years ago) and quickly became the dominant predators on Earth, forcing their relatives, the amphibians and mammal-like reptiles, into the periphery.

The Demise of the Dinosaurs

For well over 100 million years, from the mid-Triassic through the Cretaceous, dinosaurs and their kin were the dominant vertebrates on dry land. However, this was hardly a period of evolutionary stasis. Many dinosaurian families appeared and then became extinct during this time, while the dinosaurs or their reptilian friends occupied the major niches. The first birds arose from the dinosaurs in the Jurassic (~ 180 million years ago) and evolved to modern forms by the end of the Cretaceous. Throughout this time, mammals lived in a shadow of the glory of their Permian ancestors; most were restricted to tiny mouse-sized insectivores and herbivores, though a small number of species attained the size of a modern wolverine.

About 65 million years ago, at the end of the Cretaceous

period, the dinosaurs and other reptilian colleagues disappear from the fossil record. The cause of this disappearance is another of the great mysteries of geology. Part of this mystery was solved in the early 1980s when Walter and Luis Alvarez of UC Berkeley demonstrated that the Cretaceous-Tertiary boundary (known as the K-T boundary to geologists) was marked by anomalously high amounts of iridium. Iridium is a metal that is concentrated in meteorites and the core and mantle, but not the crust, of the Earth. The high iridium content of sediments at the K-T boundary indicated that the dinosaurs were snuffed out when a giant meteor struck the Earth. The discovery of a giant meteor crater, the Chicxulub crater, beneath the Cenozoic sediments on the Yucatan peninsula of Mexico confirmed this theory. This crater is 65 million years old, exactly the same age as the K-T boundary.

Geologists are fairly certain that the extinction of the dinosaurs was caused by the Chicxulub impact, but there is a considerable mystery as to why the dinosaurs were wiped out while mammals, birds, turtles, frogs, and alligators survived. One popular theory is that the killing agent from the impact was an intense but short-lived burst of thermal radiation that spread around the Earth immediately after the impact. Animals that lived in burrows, such as the small mammals, were protected when this blast roared by, as were aquatic animals, such as frogs and turtles. Unlike these smaller animals, the large dinosaurs had no such shelter and were quite literally toast.

The Radiation of the Mammals

The extinction of the dinosaurs freed the mammals from their entrapment as tiny shrew-like animals. Open forests, dense jungles, and extensive grasslands (which evolved during the Eocene) provided a wealth of open niches into which the mammals could expand. During just a few million years these shrew-like animals exploded to form an abundance of body types. Animals that we recognize as forbearers of rodents, horses, rhinoceroi, pigs, camels, elephants, and deer soon came to populate the planet. Along with them came the fearsome feline and canine predators who fed off them. As we saw earlier in the chapter, in the Eocene, another group of mammals returned to the sea to become the whales and porpoises we know today.

A small group of mammals, the primates, took up residence in the trees. While evolution caused their distant relatives to develop hooves for running on the plains, fins for swimming, or claws and jaws for efficient killing, it made changes to the primates that helped them live an arboreal life. Evolution of opposable thumbs for grasping limbs and other objects allowed them to move easily through the canopy. They developed great balance and agility that allowed them to swing easily from limb to limb. In addition they evolved sharp, binocular color vision that allowed them to see things in three dimensions and helped them to spot edible goodies within the forest canopy. All of these changes were associated with the development of a sophisticated nervous system and relatively large brain.

The Rise of Humans

In the middle Miocene (about 7 million years ago) the first ape-like creature split from the line of primates that eventually led to the old world monkeys. This animal, which was the precursor to the great apes and to humans, spread across Africa and southern Asia. In Southeast Asia its descendants eventually gave rise to orangutans, whereas in Africa they included gorillas and chimps. All three of these apes are forest dwellers. Their bodies are designed for life in the trees, for that is where they are the safest from predators. They can walk upright for short distances, but usually they support the upper portion of their body with their hands.

About 4.5 million years ago an animal appeared in Africa that was distinctly different from its ape-like cousins. This animal, which is known as *Australopithecus,* had many ape-like characteristics, including a small ape-like skull. Unlike true apes, however, it walked with an upright stance and had a human-like foot that lacked the opposable toe common in apes. These features make *Australopithecus* the first direct ancestor of humans who was not also an ancestor of apes.

A series of *Australopithecus* species appeared during the next two million years, one of which lead to the first human, *Homo habilis* (Figure 25). *Homo habilis* looked very much like *Australopithecus*; it was small with relatively long arms. However, it had a slightly larger brain. More importantly, *H. habilis* fossils are associated with primitive stone tools, something that is lacking with *Australopithecus.*

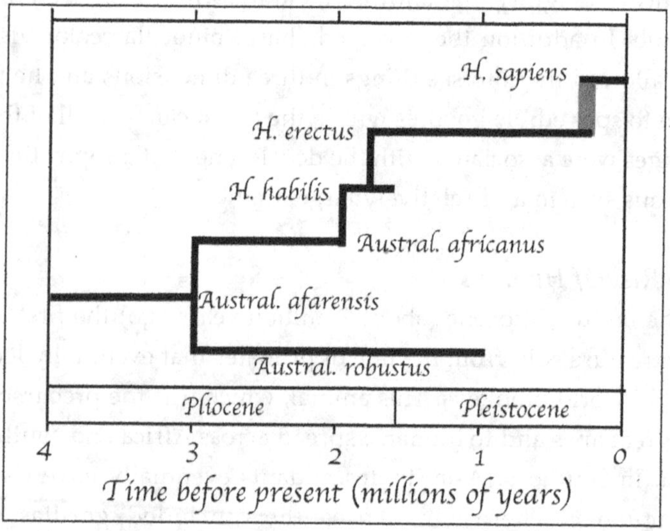

Figure 25 The evolution of humans during the last four million years. Broad gray band means that the descent from *H. erectus* to *H. sapiens* is still not well understood (see Fig. 26).

Unlike humans, who have a rib cage of relatively constant diameter, *Australopithecus* had a funnel-shaped rib cage that tapered upward. This is similar to what is seen in the great apes; the wider base is designed to accommodate a large intestinal system. This suggests that, like the great apes, *Australopithecus* had mostly a vegetarian diet. Humans have a much smaller intestinal system because we have come to live on a diet that is richer in meat, which requires less processing in the intestines. The transition from *Australopithecus* to *Homo* thus involved both the addition of meat to the diet and the use of stone tools.

Homo habilis was soon replaced by larger hominids with more evolved brain capacities. A large number of names have been proposed for these species, but recent studies show that many of the late Pliocene and Pleistocene hominids in Africa and Asia are the same species, *Homo erectus*. Most paleoanthropologists have concluded that *Homo erectus* evolved in Africa and rapidly colonized Asia, but there are a few who contend that it arose in Asia and moved into Africa. At present the fossil record is too scant to determine which theory is correct. Regardless of its origins, *Homo erectus* appeared around 1.76 million years ago and was the dominant human species for well over a million years.

The path by which modern humans arose from *H erectus* is still a matter of considerable debate. This is because the paucity of fossils makes it difficult to determine whether the variations found within the limited number of specimens available represent a number of different species or a large variation within a single species. One distinctive species that everyone is familiar with is Neanderthal man or *Homo neanderthalensis* who lived in Europe and the Middle East about 100,000 years ago. These were the stocky, slope-browed creatures that most of us think of when we hear the word 'cave man'. Anthropologists now believe that we did not descend directly from *H. neanderthalensis* but that he was as a distant cousin. The exact details of how we are related to *H. neanderthalensis* are still poorly known. Two versions are shown in Figure 26. They are different in detail depending on whether one lumps the available fossils into a few species or splits them into a large number of them. Both models agree, however, that *Homo sapiens* first appeared in Africa about 160,000 years ago and spread from there into Europe and Asia, displacing the resident hominids in the process.

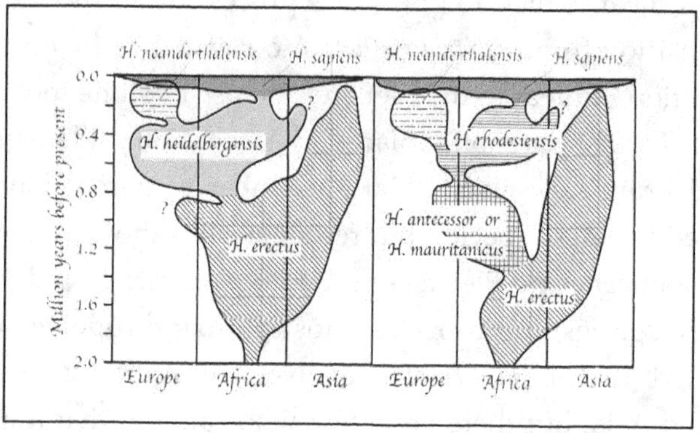

Figure 26 Two models for the evolution of modern humans[53].

The evidence compiled from fossils agrees well with conclusions obtained by studying the variation of mitochondrial RNA (mRNA) among modern human populations. These studies indicate that *Homo sapiens* arose in Africa between 150,000 and 250,000 years ago and moved into Asia, Europe, and much later Australia, the Americas, and Polynesia. Interestingly, the way that the mRNA is related in modern human populations is very similar to the way that the languages spoken by these societies are related. This strongly suggests that language developed at least 160,000 ago, which is much earlier that was assumed before the advent of mRNA dating. This means that when our ancestors left Africa they were already speaking.

Over most of its history, *Homo sapiens* made a living as nomadic hunters and gathers. Then, about 6000 years ago, a revolution in human economy began. People began to settle down in cities along the Nile and other river valleys of the Middle East and to develop agriculture. At this time the Earth was emerging from the most recent ice age and the Middle East was becoming more arid. This may have been one of the contributing factors that encouraged people to abandon their nomadic lifestyle and to settle down in the fertile bottomlands adjacent to the great rivers. Obtaining food by cultivation of plants and domestication of animals is a much more efficient way to make a living than by hunting and gathering. This allowed a sharp increase in population, which began to gather into cities. Inhabitants of these cities who were not involved in agriculture began to develop specialized professions such as carpentry and pottery and other hand-based manufacturing.

The growth of cities necessitated the development of politics and the expansion of commerce. With this new economy there also appeared a new class of people, the priests and the prophets, who were free from the need to produce food and who could turn their attention to matters of the mind. There is ample evidence that religion has been part of human culture from the very beginning, but it was only with the rise of cities that large temples tended by priests appeared. Shortly later philosophy, and eventually science, appeared as intellectual enterprises. The interaction between these various endeavors allowed human culture to evolve rapidly, with the result that only 200 to 300 generations separates the development of the first cities from the exploration of space.

The Development of the Human Brain and Consciousness

The brain capacity of hominids underwent an amazing growth during the evolution from *H. habilis* to *H. sapiens*. In only two million years the brain capacity of hominids tripled (Figure 27). The rate of this change was not constant; it seems to have been somewhat slower in the period of 1.7 to 0.6 million years ago than earlier and later. There has actually been a slight decrease in absolute brain size in the last 30,000 years (from around 1500 cc to 1300 cc). This is in response to the general decrease in human body size that is probably caused by the warming of the climate.

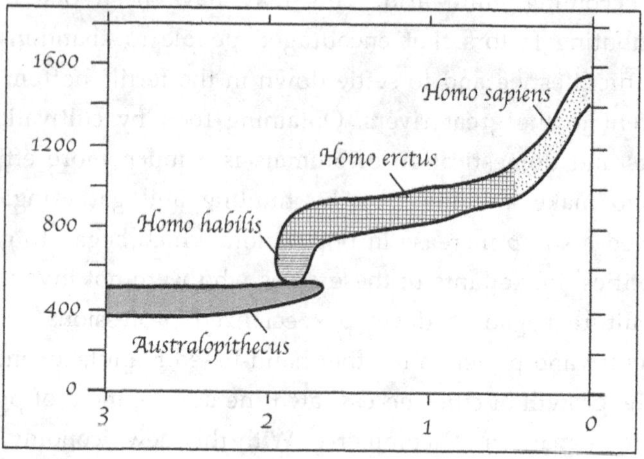

Figure 27 Diagram showing the change in cranial capacity in hominids during the past 3 million years[54].

This explosion in brainpower probably is related to the fact that our ancestors were the first creatures that relied upon tools for survival. Tools (mainly as weapons) were necessary to obtain meat, and they were the only things that kept early hominids from being food for some rather nasty predators. Clearly the cleverer a hominid was with tools, the greater were his or her chances of survival. Since the brain controlled one's cleverness with tools, with the appearance of tools there arose a strong evolutionary selection for beings with larger brains.

At what point during this great change in brain size did humans become self-conscious? When did they become aware that they existed as an independent organism and that they, like all other organisms around them, were fated to die? This is a very difficult question to answer from the fossil record. Sue Parker and Kathleen Gibson established a model for the development of ancient hominids by comparing the behavior shown by various modern apes with the cognitive development of children and with the fossil evidence of tool use.[55] They concluded that cognitive development of Australopithecans was about that of a two year old, *H. Habilis* that of a 5 to 6 year old, *Homo erectus* a 6 to 8 year old and early *H. sapiens* that of a 12 year old. In this model, self-consciousness may have been present, in a rudimentary way at least, in *H. erectus*. The brain of *H. erectus* was sufficiently complex to support speech, though there is no way that we can know whether they could speak. It is possible to envision self-consciousness in a being without speech, but it is difficult to see how speech could develop in a population without a sense of self. We know that our earliest ancestors could speak 160,000 years ago, so it is reasonable to conclude that this is the latest time at which self-consciousness could have developed.

Of course we cannot know what the people 160,000 years ago talked about. Our only hint of this comes from the elaborate cave art that appeared in many places in Europe about 35,000 years ago. This cave art is not very different from the rock art produced by the Australian Aborigines. The aborigines, who moved into Australia about 30,000 years ago, are among the last surviving example of Paleolithic culture. They have an elaborate oral tradition that involves stories of both the real world and the dreamtime. Their dreamtime stories are meant to answer questions of how humans relate to the world and how the world and the creatures that inhabit it came to be. It is not a far stretch to assume that the people who drew the cave painting were asking the same questions. Thus, it is reasonable to assume that for the past 30,000 years, and most likely for a good deal longer, humans have been asking the same questions: 'How did we get here?', 'Why are we here?' These, of course, are the very questions that make up the core of the great evolution debate.

PART III

METAPHYSICAL IMPLICATIONS

Chapter 11
The Creationists' Dilemma

Why are Creationists so Opposed to the Concept of Evolution?

In the previous five chapters of the book I have shown that the evidence for extreme antiquity of the Earth is overwhelming. I have also shown that, in addition to biology, one has to rely on many other sciences to produce a coherent story of the evolution of life on Earth. Thus, when the Creationists affirm that life on Earth is exactly as it was when God created it only a few thousand years ago, they are not merely questioning the veracity of Darwin's theory of evolution. They are also asking us to ignore all the scientific knowledge that has been accumulated over the past two centuries. How is it that in the face of all this evidence Creationists deny that evolution could have occurred?

Many scientists believe Creationists are an uneducated rabble who cling to their superstitious beliefs, despite the overwhelming evidence to the contrary. Consider the following quotes from two recent books, both of which propose that there is no conflict between Darwinism and Christianity:

> As a matter of fact, not a necessity of logic, the activists of the creationist movement against the teaching of evolution have been young-earth fundamentalists who believe that the Bible must be literally true, that the earth cannot be more than ten thousand years old, and that God created all species, separately and *ex nihilo,* in six days of twenty-four hours. These people then display a form of ultimate hubris (or maybe simple ignorance) in equating these marginal and long-discredited factual claims with the entire domain of religion.[56]

> Our powers of sense and of reason are given to us by God...and to turn our back on such firmly established science is theologically unacceptable. Not just theologically unacceptable, of course, but threatening to science, in the sense that if one's Christianity is such that one can disregard such strong science, then one's religion allows a luxury of interpretation and denial that no scientist (including a Darwinian) could permit without compromising important standard.[57]

In their arguments against Creationism, Steven J. Gould and Michael Ruse, the authors of the quotes above, maintain that there is no conflict between Darwinism and Christianity because Fundamentalists, who make up the radical fringe of the religion, don't really understand the nature of 'true' Christianity.

Gould and Ruse may well be correct. Both authors appeared as expert witnesses in the 1981 case against the Arkansas law granting equal time for teaching of Darwinism and Creationism, and hence they have first-hand experience in the debate between Evolution and Creationism. However, dismissing your opponent as incompetent is a very shoddy way to engage a debate. For this reason I endeavor to take a different approach in this book. I will begin by assuming that the arguments presented by the Creationists *are* logical. It is just that the logic they use may be different from what scientists are used to.

As we noted in Chapter 5, the root of religious faith is experience. I contend that the basis of the Creationists' opposition to evolution ultimately derives from their experience that we are surrounded by a loving presence and this experience gives an ultimate purpose to life. Unfortunately, there appears to be no room for this experience in the materialistic view of reality that is espoused by many scientists. Because there is no room in the 'scientific' worldview for their religious experience, Creationists believe that scientists must see only a small portion of reality. Furthermore, because Creationists have achieved their religious experience by following a literal interpretation of the Bible, they are convinced that the Bible is literally true. As a result, they conclude that the explanation for the origin of Earth as presented in the Bible must be true, even if it is not clear just how it is so.

The Creationists' Dilemma

The major problem Creationists face is how to address the yawning gap between their experience of reality and the materialistic view presented by modern science. Because the difference between their worldview and that of materialistic science is starkest in the field of evolution, it is here that they have concentrated their efforts. The problem that Creationists face in attacking this theory is formidable. As I showed in part II of this book, in the nearly 150 years since the publication of *The Origin of the Species* the scientific establishment has arranged a powerful array of facts and observations in support of evolution. To disprove evolution, Creationists must dismiss all of those observations. Christian Fundamentalists have evolved a variety of strategies ranging from Young-Earth Creationism to Intelligent Design to deal with this problem.

One way is to attack the veracity of the scientific story of evolution. We frequently hear Creationists say that the theory of evolution 'has holes that are so big you could drive a truck through them.' On the surface this seems a valid comment because it is clear from the previous section of the book that scientists cannot agree on most points in the story of evolution. To name a few, there are multiple explanations for the identity of the lowest universal common ancestor (LUCA), the processes of how life arose on Earth, and the causes of the Cambrian explosion. To a non-scientist this certainly can look like a great weakness, but to me, as a scientist, this is an indication that the study of evolution is still a vibrant field. Thirty-five years ago, when I received my Ph.D., there were major holes in our understanding of the history of life on Earth. Science had virtually no explanation for the Cambrian explosion or for the great extinction of the dinosaurs. At that time, the scientific story of early evolution was very simple – life evolved somehow in a primordial soup. The details were thin. Since then, scientists have made amazing progress. They have discovered that the composition of ocean floor sediments show a major change from anoxic to oxygenated at the Cambrian boundary and today a solid story of how the Cambrian explosion occurred is beginning to emerge. They discovered that a meteorite impact at the end of the Cretaceous probably snuffed out the dinosaurs. In addition, they have made great advances in the study of early evolution. They have discovered the complexities of the microbiological world, the abundance of life in ocean floor vents, and how to use rRNA to further dissect the history of evolution. The disparate stories that scientists have come up with over the past few decades to explain early evolution are a result of all these new techniques and findings.

What we see today in the study of evolution is a snapshot of science in progress. If you were to look at the field of chemistry in 1860, about the time the Frederick Kekulé was working on the structure of benzine, you would have found it similarly contentious. There were many theories of chemical thermodynamics and ways chemical compounds are put together. Over the years those theories that did not explain the observations have died away, with the result that looking back nearly 150 years later, the history of chemistry looks like a smooth and linear process. In a similar way, it may take a few more decades before dead-end theories about the origin of life and early evolution fall away and all the conflicting data are combined into a grand unifying story of evolution.

When Creationists use the disputes among scientists as a reason to disregard the theory of evolution, they seldom point out that these conflicts are only over the details of the process. The scientists don't dispute that evolution is a fact, that the Earth is 4560 million years old; that the Earth was barren when it formed, and that all life on Earth has evolved from a common ancestor. The disputes are over how life originated and the details over how it evolved. Thus, when Creationists argue that evolution didn't occur because scientists cannot agree on HOW it occurred, they are using a very weak argument indeed.

In addition to discounting the scientific method in general, Young-Earth Creationists dismiss the scientific evidence for the antiquity of the Earth by arguing that physical laws are not constant and that time flowed at a different rate immediately after creation than it does now. In other words, the Earth *appears* old to geologists because isotopic clocks moved very fast in the first years of the Earth. The problem with this explanation is that the radioactive reactions that form the geological clocks also produce a lot of heat. If the Earth is really only 10,000 years old and the radioactive elements only appear to be old because they initially decayed very rapidly, then the heat released by this decay would have melted the Earth. This is an event that surely would have been mentioned in the Bible.

Another way that Young-Earth Creationists deal with the problem of geologic time is by arguing that it is illusionary. Since Adam was an adult when God created him, why couldn't the Earth be 4500 million years old when God made it? There is nothing wrong with this worldview per se and there is no reason why one cannot use it as a means for constructing one's spiritual life. The problem comes in applying this argument to science, as Young-Earth Creationists wish to do. The argument that the Earth only appears old because God made it that way clearly relies on a supernatural interpretation for the phenomenal world, which of course contradicts the naturalistic underpinnings of science. As I noted back in Chapter 2, science cannot exist without a naturalistic view of the world. There should be little surprise, therefore, that scientists react apoplectically when Young-Earth Creationists advocate teaching this in a science class, for it carries a message that completely denies the validity of the scientific method.

The Intelligent Design Creationists soften the arguments of the Young-Earth Creationists somewhat by accepting the antiquity of the Earth, but they argue that some biochemical processes are so complex that they could have only arisen by Intelligent Design.[58] However, the fact that the advocates of Intelligent Design provide no explanation of how this Intelligent Design works weakens these arguments considerably.[59] Scientists also maintain that the arguments of Intelligent Design theory are crippled because they call upon a supernatural cause to explain problems that seem intractable. Just because a process is beyond our comprehension at the moment doesn't mean that further work will not illuminate a naturalistic cause for it. What would have happened to the history of chemistry if in the mid-nineteenth century Kekulé said to himself, 'Gee, the structure of benzene is just too complex for us to understand. I guess God just made it that way. Maybe I should work on something easier.'

The Creationists' Strategies

As the discussion above shows, nowhere can Creationists present a positive argument in their favor. Such an argument would go 'Because of A, then B, and because of B then C, and C implies that Creationism must have occurred'. All of their positive arguments fall apart under scrutiny.[60] Because of this, Creationists have developed several other strategies to attack Darwinism. Perhaps the most standard way has been to establish that there is an either-or choice between Darwinism and Creationism. A person observing the debate must choose between either Godless Darwinism or God as embodied in Creationism. By this construction, there is no middle ground. Once this all-or-nothing premise has been established,

Creationists present a large number of arguments designed to 'show' that evolution is impossible. The intention is that once Darwinism has been shown to be false, the listener has no choice but to accept Creationism as the true answer.

Using this approach, Creationists attack evolution with a series of arguments each of which starts with 'Evolution cannot have occurred because...' At the end of this phrase, Creationists insert reasons that are 'half-truths'. What they present is truthful; however, they present ONLY those aspects of the argument that fit their purposes. When one looks into each of Creationists' arguments in detail, as has been done in numerous court cases, their apparently solid case against evolution falls apart.

The arguments using half-truths may be persuasive to someone who has no scientific background because it is much easier to dismiss a complex problem with a simple statement than it is to explain why that simple statement is wrong. Scientists have written numerous books to answer the arguments put forth by the Creationists and to show where the statements are overstated or simply wrong. A good example of this 'half truth' approach is Phillip Johnson's argument in his book *Darwin on Trial* that the 'sudden' appearance of abundant life forms in the Cambrian is clear proof that evolution couldn't have worked as Darwin envisioned it. This argument, which can be presented in a couple of simple sentences, looks devastating to Darwinism. However, as I discussed in Chapter 10, the appearance of varied life forms in the Cambrian was not as sudden as Johnson would have one believe and there are reasonable explanations for how it came about without divine intervention.

Another approach that Intelligent Design Creationists take is more sinister. In *Darwin on Trial,* Johnson maintains that scientists are part of a dogmatic cult that is using schools to push a materialistic philosophy onto an unsuspecting public. He contends that scientists don't accept the theories of Creationists because those theories threaten scientist's attempts to control society. According to this argument, scientists are closed-minded zealots who, if they were open-minded like Creationists, would see the obvious hand of a Creator in the design of life. This leads Johnson to ask, 'Why does the law protect the religion of 'science' over the open discussion of Intelligent Design?' Through this statement, Johnson implies that Creationists cannot succeed in the legal arena because scientists have infiltrated the political and legal system of the country. This is a difficult argument to deal with, because it relies upon innuendo rather than any facts. Furthermore, it is a political, rather than a scientific argument. I raise it here simply to show that, just like statements of scientists, such as those quoted at the beginning of this chapter, the tactics of many Creationists tend to poison the debate rather than illuminate it.

The Errors in the Creationist Approach

Creationists have been forced to develop these negative and ultimately unsuccessful arguments against evolution because of the interpretations they derive from their religious experience. Firstly, they mistakenly equate belief with faith. The fact that prayer opens them to spiritual experience proves that prayer is a powerful way of probing the unseen. It does not follow that it is the ONLY way to attain spiritual awakening, nor does the efficacy of prayer prove in any way that the Bible is infallible. Many passages in the Bible, such as those relating to animal sacrifice, have little relevance to modern society and have long since been discarded, even by Fundamentalists.

Secondly, their argument about Biblical infallibility confuses subjective knowledge with objective knowledge. Over the past two thousand years, it has been well established that the Bible is a useful guide toward spiritual knowledge. Spiritual knowledge is, of course, subjective knowledge and, because it is difficult to describe subjective knowledge directly, the pathway provided by the Bible is through parables and symbols. However adequately the Bible can be used to address subjective knowledge, it obviously fails when addressing objective knowledge. Most of our scientific knowledge of the world evolved thousands of years after the Bible was written. Thus, regardless of how spiritually valid the book may be, it is ludicrous to assume that the Bible has any relevance to the first law of thermodynamics, the periodic table, or computer programming. If you were building a bridge you would not consult the Bible to find the tensile strength of steel. Likewise, if a pharmacist told you that she had concocted your heart medicine according to a formula in the Bible, chances are you would start looking for another pharmacist. Similarly, we can conclude that the Bible has no relevance at all to the age of the Earth.

Ironically, the Fundamentalists are correct in their contention that the materialism engendered by science is terribly one-sided. The stand they take against the materialistic view proposed by many scientists about the significance of life is valid and incredibly important. Unfortunately, the approaches they use in their battles against evolution are counterproductive for two reasons. Firstly, they set a very negative tone. This is partially because of the negative arguments that they are forced to use and partially because authors such as Phillip Johnson impute ulterior motives to scientists that simply are not true. This negativism puts Creationists in a very poor light and makes it easy for scientists to dismiss their arguments, despite the fact that they raise valid concerns over the materialistic worldview of science.[61]

The second problem is that Creationists base their arguments upon a very limited view of religion and spirituality. Part of their disgust with evolution comes from the fact that, if life evolved by natural processes, it negates the need for a Creator. The existence of a Creator is key to someone reading the Bible literally, which explains the passion that drives Creationists to fight Darwinism. However, as I noted in Chapter 5, a literal creator is not a critical aspect to all religions; a belief in a Creator is not even a necessary tenet in Christianity.[62] By concentrating on Biblical infallibility, the Creationists limit their arguments to a very restricted field, one that is poorly defensible against naturalistic arguments.

The view of humanity constructed by materialists in the name of science presents a number of problems that should be a concern to people of all faiths. Interestingly, Fundamentalist Christians seem to be the only religious group to address the emptiness that materialism presents. Unfortunately, the approach taken by the Creationists to the debate obscures most of these problems and reduces the question simply to a matter of belief. Before we can have any hope of finding a common ground between science and religion, we have to define the problems in a way that avoids the venom and toxicity that has characterized the debate up to now. This is what I will try to do in the next three chapters.

Chapter 12
Two Views of Consciousness: The Mind-brain Problem

As the previous chapter implies, Fundamentalists attack evolution because it is presented with a materialist view that completely contradicts their deepest experience. The cold, amoral, mechanistic view inherent in materialism carries the implication that life is essentially meaninglessness. This worldview stands in utter opposition to the Christian beliefs that life has a deep meaning and that a moral life lived with a heart-felt concern for others is a key to unlocking that meaning. This clash in worldviews, more than any Biblical dogma, is the driving force for the Fundamentalist opposition to evolution.[63]

Perhaps the greatest irony in the debate over evolution is that, by attacking the objective facts of evolution, namely the age of the Earth and the evolution of species, the followers of Creationism (be it Young-Earth or Intelligent Design Creationism) are attacking the greatest strength of the materialists. As we noted in Chapter 3, science is built upon objective knowledge. Therefore, it should be no surprise that, when the debate focuses on the objective facts of evolution, the Creationists end up getting soundly trounced. However, often lost in the debate between Creationism and Evolution is the fact that materialism has an Achilles Heel. This weakness lies in the fact that science cannot explain the nature and origin of consciousness.

One of the reasons why the evolution debate is so vitriolic is that biology, unlike physics, chemistry, geology, and astronomy, extends from the field of material objects into the realm of life. As such, it must deal with consciousness. Although fish or proto-zoans may not be conscious, humans certainly are and many mammals show some signs of consciousness as well. Science, however, has a very difficult time determining where consciousness comes from and whether animals other that humans are conscious.

Even defining consciousness is extremely difficult to do. We know that consciousness somehow is associated with our sense of 'me'. This 'me' is something seemingly living within our mind that is aware of the experiences the body has encountered. Memories of these experiences seem to reside in 'me' and assemble themselves to form our personalities. In addition, 'me' carries with it a sense of volition. It has the ability to develop needs and desires and to direct the behavior of the body in ways that are designed to fulfill these needs. Finally, 'me' seems to be continually churning out vivid stories, images, and emotions. Many times we are more aware of the stories that this 'me' is telling us than we are of the world 'out there'. Although we have these impressions of what consciousness *does*, we find it very difficult to define what it *is*. Of course, we shouldn't feel too badly about our inability to grasp the nature of consciousness, for this is a problem that has troubled philosophers for more than 2,500 years.

Philosophical Views on the Nature of Consciousness

The numerous schools of thought that have arisen to describe the nature of consciousness fit into two groups: dualism and monism. Monism itself has been divided into materialism and idealism.

Dualism

Dualistic philosophical schools hold that consciousness arises from something that is different from the material world. Dualism is inherent in Christian theology, wherein a spiritual God stands apart from our material bodies. This theory was most clearly set forth by the French philosopher René Descartes (1596-1650). Descartes argued that there is a distinction between mental and physical substances. He noted that the defining characteristic of matter is that it occupies space, whereas the defining characteristic of the mind is consciousness. This is the concept behind his famous quotation 'cogito ergo sum'; *I think, therefore I am.* The fact that Descartes was conscious proved that he existed.

In addition to defining dualism, Descartes tried to address the major problem with dualism; How is it that an external consciousness and a material brain interact? Descartes contended that this interaction took place in the pineal gland, a small mass with glandular properties located deep in folds of the brain. This contention was shown to be wrong long ago, and most modern materialists would maintain that the question of how the spiritual world (if they allow that it exists) interacts with the material one is still one of the biggest problems in dualism.

Materialism

If the material world and the world of consciousness are not composed of two different substances, then they must be of the same substance. This field of philosophy is called *monism,* a school that maintains there is but one substance that gives rise both to bodies and to consciousness. In Western society, the most commonly held school of monism is materialism, which contends that consciousness arises in some way out of material 'stuff'. This was first stated explicitly by Julien Offray de La Mettrie (1709-1751). In his book, *L'homme machine* (1747), he maintained, as indicated by the book's title, that our consciousness is produced by activities with our brain. Le Mettrie noted that animal tissue might continue to move when separated from the central nervous system and suggested that this intrinsic power of motion was sufficient to explain consciousness. We now know that this 'intrinsic motion' is due to electrical activity of autonomic nerves and has little to do with consciousness. The question that Le Mettrie tried to answer, how material stuff can become conscious, is, of course, the major problem of materialism. Volumes of Western philosophy have been written on this question.

Idealism

The other type of monism is idealism. In contrast to materialism, idealism maintains that the mind is the basis of reality and that the physical world exists only as a manifestation of the mind. The term 'idealism' covers a wide range of concepts. On one end of the spectrum is simple skepticism that carries no spiritual implications. Such schools of idealism simply aver that all we can know of physical objects is how they present themselves to our senses. On the other end stands the schools holding that the essence of reality is the 'One' that is absolutely beyond concept. Schools on this side of the spectrum include Neoplatonism, as exemplified by the teachings of the Roman philosopher Plotinus (205-270 CE), the Advaita monism of Hinduism, which maintains that all is one in Brahma, and the teachings of the Chittamatra (or Mind-Only school) of Mahayana Buddhism.

The Scientific View of Consciousness

Cognitive Science, the scientific field that studies consciousness, is unabashedly materialistic. Consider the following statement by Daniel Dennett, whose 1991 book, *Consciousness Explained,* carries a title that humbly implies that he has finally solved the problem that had stumped philosophers for nearly two millennia:

> The prevailing wisdom, variously expressed and argued for, is *materialism:* there is only one sort of stuff, namely *matter* – the physical stuff of physics, chemistry, physiology – and the mind is somehow nothing but a physical phenomenon. In short the mind is the brain. According to materialists we can (in principle!) account for every mental phenomenon using the same physical principles, laws and raw materials that suffice to explain radioactivity, continental drift, photosynthesis, reproduction, nutrition, and growth.[64]

Modern studies of neurophysiology have strongly supported this view that consciousness is merely the chemical and electrical activity of the brain (see the quote from Francis Crick in Chapter 2). When people experience various emotions and thoughts, neurophysiologists have identified that electrical activity will be concentrated in different areas of the brain. In fact, some neurologists have even recognized an area of the brain that is active during transcendental experiences. With their comment that 'there is no other way for God to get into your head except through the brain's neural pathways', neurologists developed a new field of science they call neurotheology, a completely materialistic model for the religious experience.[65]

There are two major problems with the approaches that cognitive scientists take to understanding consciousness. Firstly, they mix up naturalism and materialism. As I noted in Chapters 2 and 3, it is entirely valid for science to take a naturalistic of the world. Without doing so, science has no way to dissect rigorously the behavior of natural phenomena. However, just because naturalism can effectively describe the physical world, it is not valid to assume that science proves that reality is *limited* to the physical world. In other words, nothing in science *proves* the validity of a materialistic view of the world, not the least of which is due to the fact that science cannot *prove* anything! As I noted in Chapter 4, the scientific method can disprove theories, but it cannot prove them. In most fields of science, a reasonable scientist may stay away from this philosophical tangle. However, as soon as science begins to deal with consciousness, as does cognitive science, it is implicitly (if not explicitly) embracing materialism.

The second problem is that, by assuming one can measure consciousness by looking at electrical activity in the brain, scientists confuse objective knowledge with subjective knowledge. Consciousness is an intensely subjective experience; in fact, one could say that it is the cause of all our subjective experiences.

Consciousness is not an object; it is not something that can be touched, measured or weighed. As such, it exists beyond the limits of scientific examination. Therefore, the quotes by Crick and Dennett cited above, rather than being scientific statements, are declarations of a belief that differs little from the contention Creationists make that the Earth was created only 6,000 years ago.

Two Views on the Importance of Consciousness

The way one views the relationship between mind and matter determines the importance one gives to consciousness in the world. Materialists consider that matter is the most important stuff in the universe; consciousness is restricted to the domain of humans and, perhaps, to a lesser extent, to a few other advanced mammals (Figure 28A). Irrespective of whether consciousness stands apart from matter, as dualists would contend, or whether it pervades matter, as idealists would maintain, dualists and idealists concur in the assertion that consciousness is the most important stuff in the universe (Figure 28B). This, of course, is the contention that all religions hold, regardless of the details of their dogma (see Chapter 5).

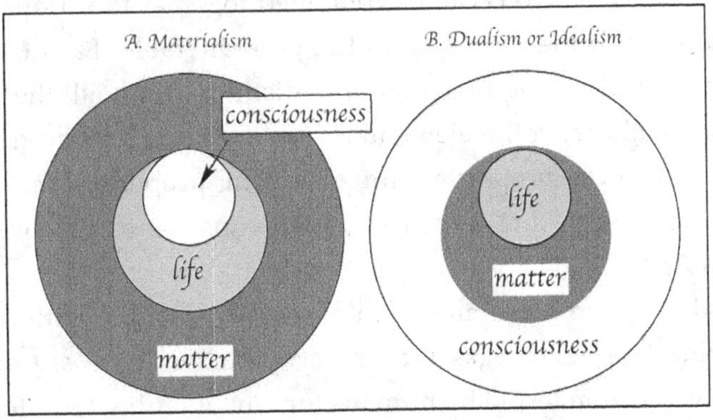

Figure 28 The relationship between consciousness and matter as viewed by the concepts of: A. Materialism or B. Dualism or Idealism.

Not surprisingly, one's view of the relationship between mind and matter also determines how one views the role that consciousness plays in evolution. To a materialist, consciousness is an *emergent* epiphenomenon; it is a product of chemical reactions in our brains that has emerged as neurological systems became more complex. In contrast, if one holds either a dualistic or idealistic view, then consciousness has *transcendent* properties.

Consciousness as an Emergent Epiphenomenon

One of the core observations in science is that as a system grows more complex, properties arise that were not present when it was in a simpler state. Such properties are called *emergent properties*, and they are present at all levels of the cosmos.[66] For example, all electrons in the universe have the identical mass and electrical charge. The same can be said for protons and neutrons. However, when one electron is bonded to one proton in a certain way, an entirely new substance is produced, namely hydrogen. Hydrogen has a slightly lower mass than the total mass of a free electron and proton. In addition, it has a host of chemical properties, such as a melting point and a boiling point, that have no meaning when applied to electrons or protons. Electrons, protons, and neutrons can be combined together in various ways to produce all the elements on the periodic table. Each element has chemical properties that are distinct from all the other elements and from the elementary particles that produced them. These chemical properties are emergent properties that arise from the way that electrons, neutrons, and protons are assembled.

Sodium is a light metal that reacts violently with water. Chlorine is a yellow gas that is very reactive. Both are deadly poisons when ingested by humans (or any other life form for that matter). However, when sodium (Na) and chlorine (Cl) are combined, they produce NaCl, common table salt. Salt, in small portions at least, is not poisonous, but conversely is vital for life.

The combination of these two elements produces a compound that has emergent properties (such as taste and solubility) that are not present in the elements themselves. Table 3 gives a list of substances and the emergent properties that arise with increasing complexity. Some of the properties in the lower classes are present in the higher classes, though others are not. For example, application of the idea of electrical charge to a compound like NaCl, or much worse to a mouse is ridiculous.

Interestingly, each transition to a more complex substance also involves a transition to a different field of science (Table 3). Thus, physics is the field that studies the properties of sub-atomic particles, but once these particles have been amassed into atoms their study becomes the realm of chemistry. This occurs because reductionist techniques defined for one level of

Table 3
Emergent properties

Substance	*Elementary particles*	*Elements*	*Compounds*	*Organisms*	*Consciousness*
Emergent properties	*charge mass*	*melting and boiling points, valance*	*bonding, solubility, acidity*	*life, reproduction, metabolism*	*awareness, insight, creativity, intuition*
Field of Science	*Physics*	*Chemistry*		*Biology*	*Phschology*
	Increasing complexity →				

complexity do not work well when applied to phenomena that have a higher level of complexity. The more complex phenomena will have emergent properties that cannot be predicted from the behavior of simpler systems. For example, quantum mechanics can be used to explain many phenomena dealing with sub-atomic particles, but it is nearly useless in answering the question: 'What would the composition of the atmosphere be if it was in equilibrium with rocks containing native iron?' To answer this question, one must use chemical thermodynamics, a field that is only distantly related to quantum mechanics. Similarly, chemical thermodynamics would be useless if the question we wished to answer was 'How are birds related to dinosaurs?' Thus, although all fields of science take a similar approach to answering the questions they encounter, they each have evolved different techniques for probing the emergent properties that are unique to their field of study.

Life is an emergent property. We all know that life forms are made up of a series of complex organic chemical compounds. However, even the simplest bacterium in a drop of swamp water is much more than merely the sum of all the proteins and organic compounds from which it is made. It is alive. It has the ability to obtain nutrients from its surroundings and to extract energy from them by way of metabolism. In addition, it is able to reproduce (almost) exact copies of itself. These properties that we consider to be characteristic of life can, therefore, also be considered as emergent properties. This is the reason why the question of how life began is so intractable. Scientists can model the processes that may have lead to the formation of life, but so far, duplicating the emergent property of life itself has proven elusive.

With this background, it is logical to conclude that consciousness is nothing but an emergent epiphenomenon of living beings. As vertebrates evolved from fish to mammals, the brain became increasingly complex. Reasoning would tell us that consciousness is such a complicated process that it cannot manifest itself until a creature obtains a minimum of synapses within its brain. Most scientists would admit that the higher mammals have some rudimentary form of consciousness, but that consciousness didn't attain its full flowering until the brain underwent the huge increase in size during the evolution of humans. According to this view, consciousness, difficult though it may be to define, is simply an epiphenomenon that arose late in the history of evolution. As such, consciousness has only minimal importance to the whole scheme of things (Figure 28).

Consciousness as a Transcendent Property

As we noted in Chapter 5, all religions consider that there is an aspect of consciousness that resides outside of our bodies, i.e. that is transcendent. This transcendent aspect of consciousness, which in this book I have called Ultimate Reality, is given different names by various traditions: God or Jehovah in the Jewish and Christian traditions, Allah in Islam, Brahma by the Hindus. The Buddhists maintain that the transcendent aspect of consciousness is beyond concept and generally give it no name at all. Whatever name one uses, as we noted in Chapter 5, religions maintain that Ultimate Reality manifests in our life as consciousness.

Those who contend that aspects of consciousness are transcendental agree that human self-consciousness is an emergent phenomenon. They would maintain, however, that the emergent property is not the ability to produce consciousness, as implied by the materialists, but the ability to access something that already is there. In this view, the chemical and electrical activities in our brains, important though they may be, are not the ultimate sources of consciousness. This contention that consciousness is not seated in the brain seems counter-intuitive to many people (particularly materialists like Crick and Dennett). Even discounting the modern studies of human cognition, there are good reasons to conclude that consciousness is a product of activity within the brain. Most of us know of people who have had brain damage produced by an accident, stroke, or Alzheimer's disease. Depending on the extent of the damage, these people show varying degrees of disability, from mild aphasia through dementia to complete unconsciousness.

Rather than *assuming* that all of consciousness is produced within the brain, religious people contend that some aspect of consciousness is derived from outside the body. In other words, rather than the brain being able to produce consciousness, as implied by materialists, religious people maintain that it is also a receiver of consciousness. Thus, the fact that stimulation of the temporal lobe of the brain can induce transcendent experiences does not mean that the religious experience is simply a chemical reaction. Thus, religious people have a simple answer to the rather derisive comments of cognitive scientist David Noelle:

> How do you know that your religious experience is not a simple trick of your brain – the unfolding of a perfectly natural temporal lobe transient? How can you trust such an experience when, through science, we can convincingly mimic the face of God?[67]

Stimulation of the temporal lobes affects how one views his or her self, and as I noted in Chapter 5, once you drop the sense of self, Ultimate Reality reveals itself to you. There is no way Noelle (or anyone else) can prove that the stimulation of this part of the brain *produces* transcendent experiences rather than simply *opens* one to them.

A good analogy to your brain might be your TV. If one of the circuits in your TV malfunctions, the TV reception will suffer in a way that is very similar to a person with brain damage. The TV image might be jittery and fuzzy, or there might be no image at all. However, just because you can tie the cause of the bad reception to problems in the TV circuitry, you certainly wouldn't maintain that the TV show was produced within your TV set. Equating neurophysiology to the study of consciousness is equivalent to looking at the activities of the circuits in the back of the TV to determine whether the show being projected on the screen is *Hamlet* or *Gilligan's Island.* To be more extreme, to maintain that we understand the source of consciousness because we understand where the brain responds to stimuli is like looking in the back to the TV set to determine from what city the TV show is being broadcast.

Metaphysical Implications

The question of whether consciousness is a transcendent or an emergent property is more than just a simple question of philosophy. How one views the nature of consciousness plays a critical role in determining where one places humanity in the world. If consciousness is merely an emergent epiphenomenon of life, then it really plays only a minor role in the main scheme of things (Figure 28A). This view carries depressing implications. It reduces all the wonder and beauty of life to meaningless electrical impulses in your head. What's more, it implies that life itself is basically meaningless: the wealth of thoughts and concepts that populate our minds will evaporate when our brains turns off at death. In the words of Bertrand Russell:

> That man is the product of causes which had no prevision of the end they were achieving; that his origin, his growth, his hopes and fears, his loves and beliefs, are but the outcome of accidental collections of atoms; that no fire, no heroism, no intensity of thought and feeling, can preserve an individual life beyond the grave; that all the labours of the ages, all the devotion, all the inspiration, all the noonday brightness of human genius, are destined to extinction in the vast death of the solar system, and the whole temple of Man's achievement must inevitably be buried beneath the debris of a universe in ruins – all these things, if not quite beyond dispute, are yet so nearly certain, that no philosophy which rejects them can hope to stand.[68]

According to the materialistic view, our major goal in life is to pass our genes on to our offspring, and after that has been done we are essentially worthless and taking up resources that are needed by the important breeding stock of the species.

In contrast, if one accepts the view that consciousness is transcendent, then consciousness (what we have been calling Ultimate Reality) is the most important aspect of the universe (Figure 28B). This view gives life inherent meaning because transcendent consciousness is the ultimate source of the experiences of love, creativity, awe and beauty. A good example of this worldview (and an answer to the nihilism of Bertrand Russell quoted above) comes from the introduction to Ken Wilber's masterpiece, *Sex, Ecology, and Spirituality*.

> To Schelling's burning question. 'Why is there something rather than nothing?': there have always been two general answers. The first might be called the philosophy of 'oops'. The universe just occurs, there is nothing behind it, it's all ultimately accidental or random, it just is, it just happens – oops! The philosophy of oops, no matter how sophisticated and adult it may on occasion appear – its modern names and numbers are legion, from positivism to scientific materialism, from linguistic analysis to historical materialism, from naturalism to empiricism – always comes down to the same basic answer, namely, 'Don't ask.'...
>
> The other broad answer that has been tendered is that *something else is going on*: behind the happenstance drama is a deeper or higher or wider pattern, or order, or intelligence. There are, of course many varieties of this 'Deeper Order' the Tao, God, Geist, Maat, Archetypal Forms, Reason, Li, Mahayama, Brahman, Rigpa. And although these different varieties of the Deeper Order certainly disagree with each other at many points, they all agree on this: the universe is not what it appears. *Something else* is going on, something quite other than oops...[69]

Is there any way to distinguish between these models?

The two quotes above present such a jarringly different view of reality that it is difficult to see how both of them can be correct. How can we determine which of these two views is valid? In other words, what evidence do we have that consciousness is transcendent? Over the past several thousand years religions have developed various programs to introduce their adherents to the existence of a transcendent consciousness. All you have to do is to spend a long time in prayer or meditation, or whatever approach your particular religion advocates, and the transcendent nature of consciousness will spontaneously reveal itself. This experiment has been conducted by millions of people over thousands of years, and the religious literature is full of descriptions of their experiences. Unfortunately, all these experiments are subjective (obviously!) and not reproducible (at least in the way that scientific experiments are reproducible). Hence, they are not very persuasive to people who are searching for *objective, scientific* proof (and incidentally who are not willing to subject themselves to the experiment of religious practice). Is there any objective way to determine whether consciousness is an emergent or transcendent property?

Perhaps the best objective evidence for the existence of a transcendent consciousness is what happens at death, when the neural activity in the brain ceases. If it is merely an epiphenomenon of brain activity, then the consciousness of every individual should be extinguished upon death. In contrast, if it is transcendent, then there is an aspect of our consciousness that survives death. All major religions contend that this is the case, although there is considerable disagreement as to just exactly what survives and what happens to it after death.

Striking objective evidence for the existence of transcendent consciousness comes from *near-death experiences,* often abbreviated as NDEs. These experiences are described by some patients who were resuscitated from apparent death or who experienced accidents or illnesses that brought them close to death. In his classic book on near-death experiences, Raymond Moody recorded fifteen features that are common in NDEs, although no person describing an NDE encountered all these experiences.[70]

Early on in the near-death experience the patient hears a

buzzing noise and is aware of moving through a dark tunnel. He (or she) emerges from the tunnel to find himself outside his physical body, watching medical efforts to resuscitate him. Often this person finds himself observing the process from above and behind the doctors who are working on his physical body. This perception would be impossible if it were originating in some way from within the body. After a while, the person experiencing the NDE moves on, often in company with relatives who have died previously. She (or he) comes to a warm, loving being, often called a being of light, who asks her questions to evaluate her life. Toward the end of the experience, the patient is told that it is not her time to die and quickly thereafter she finds herself back in her body.

People with a religious background maintain that NDEs are strong evidence that something within the mind survives death. Materialists, however, contend that there are alternative explanations for this phenomenon. Their first comment is that the person describing an NDE was not dead; otherwise they would not have returned. After all, none of the patients described in the initial reports of NDEs had EEGs that would prove that the brain activity had ceased during the time of their NDEs. However, recently a report has been published that describes a woman who had a vivid NDE during surgery for a massive brain aneurism.[71] During this surgery the patient's blood was circulated through a heart-lung machine and cooled. After the body had cooled sufficiently, the blood was drained from her brain and the aneurism was tied off. When the blood was drained from her brain her EEG went flat; there was no brain action at all. Despite the flat EEG the patient experienced a profound NDE during the surgery and could describe accurately events that took place during the time when the EEG indicated nothing was going on in her brain.

Materialist and skeptics dismiss the NDE described above because it relies on 'the unsupported testimony of the author' (who was the doctor performing the surgery). This is a very typical approach that materialists take toward NDEs; rather than discussing the subjective experiences of the patients, they deny that the experience has any significance at all because it wasn't studied rigorously enough. Here the materialists mistake subjective knowledge with objective knowledge and assume that, since we cannot derive objective proof for subjective experiences, those experiences are invalid. What the skeptics of NDEs cannot explain is that an NDE has a far more profound effect on the patient than does a simple hallucination. Patients who have had an NDE find that it leads to a greater appreciation for life, an increased interest in spirituality, and an increase in empathy for others.

In another strange feature associated with dying, many patients suffering from terminal illnesses undergo unusual experiences as death approaches. This includes experiencing the presence of unseen beings, some of whom may be acquaintances who have died earlier, feeling a sense that he or she is getting ready to leave, seeing a place where they will be going after death, and knowing when death will take place. Patricia Kelley and Maggie Callanan, two hospice nurses who observed these experiences many times among their patients, called this phenomenon *nearing death awareness.*[72] Interestingly, this awareness is just as likely to be developed in a patient who is an atheist as in one with a strong religious background. Like the NDEs, the nearing death awareness presents a view of reality that is totally inexplicable by the materialistic view of the world, and hence is usually dismissed by most materialists.

The materialistic view of reality is particularly challenged by the unusual phenomena that accompany the death of enlightened religious figures. The most famous example of this would be the disappearance of Jesus' body. After the crucifixion, Jesus' body is said to have been wrapped in linen and placed into a stone tomb that was sealed with a great boulder. When the boulder was removed three days later, the linen was there but the body was gone. Materialists would argue that this is simply a fairy tale, and certainly the descriptions we have of the event were written down decades after it occurred. It would be reasonable to ignore the story of Jesus' disappearance, were it not for the fact that similar spectacular events have accompanied the deaths of enlightened lamas in ancient India and Tibet. Their bodies are reported to have dissolved into light upon death in a phenomenon known as a 'rainbow body'.[73] Unfortunately, such singular occurrences have either occurred in the distant past or in remote regions; hence, it is impossible to evaluate the veracity of these reported events.

Although we have no way of substantiating (or refuting) the stories of rainbow bodies, there is other evidence suggesting that death involves more than merely pulling the plug on the neural activity of your brain. Unusual things have happened during (or after) the deaths of a large number of highly trained practitioners in the Eastern Religions.[74] Perhaps the most striking phenomenon is called death-samadhi, in which the bodies of advanced meditation practitioners can remain warm for hours or even weeks after brain death. Often the warmth remains concentrated in the heart region while the extremities become cold. Dozens of these events have been described in the literature of Eastern Religion, but the best-recorded example of death-samadhi is the death of the sixteenth Gyalwang Karmapa in 1981.[75]

The Karmapa is the head of the Kagyü lineage of Tibetan Buddhism and, as such, holds a position equivalent to that of the Dalai Lama, who in addition to being the head of state is the head of the Geluk lineage. In 1981, the sixteenth Karmapa, who was suffering from the latest stages of cancer, was taken to AMER International Hospital in Zion, Illinois. After a few days in the hospital he fell into deepening shock in response to extensive internal bleeding. The condition became so bad that the doctor treating him announced to his attendants that the Karmapa had only hours to live. A few moments later the bleeding stopped, the Karmapa's blood pressure returned to normal, and he sat up in bed as if nothing had happened. This astounded the medical staff because never before had they seen a person recover from such a grave condition. Nine or ten days later, the Karmapa's condition deteriorated again. He had a massive infection, extensive internal bleeding, and falling blood pressure; a condition that is uniformly fatal. Again, the doctor in charge announced that death was imminent and again the Karmapa seemed to come back from the brink. The bleeding stopped and his vital signs became normal.

Finally, two days later, the Karmapa died. However, his death did not follow any pattern expected by modern medicine. The area around his heart remained warm for three days, and throughout this time, his skin and muscles retained their normal tension. Even two days after he had died, there was no sign of rigor mortis, which usually sets in 2 to 12 hours after death. The monks in the Karmapa's entourage explained to the doctors that though he was dead, the Karmapa's consciousness was still occupying the body and that decay would not set in until the consciousness had left. After three days, the death-samadhi ended, the body became cold, and rigor mortis set in. Within a few hours, the corpse became as decayed as a normal body would have been had it been dead for three days.

There are three ways we can respond to the mysteries related to death and dying. We can use them to support our religious faith, as millions around the world do. We can discount them as being insignificant phenomena because the stories that describe them simply are not scientific observations. Because they are not scientific, we may argue that they cannot be considered truthful. The third way is to acknowledge that the world may be more complex than we have assumed it to be and remain open to the possibility that aspects of consciousness are transcendent rather than emergent. I urge the reader to hold this third view in the next two chapters as we examine the implications that the presence of a transcendent consciousness would have on our views of evolution.

Chapter 13
Two Views of Evolution

Evolutionary Materialism

As I noted in Chapter 2, the scientific revolution has shown that simple physical laws can explain the phenomenal world of chemistry and physics. We no longer need to call upon Divine intervention to explain lightning, rainbows, or earthquakes. Darwin extended this concept into the realm of biology. He showed that the evolution of species, and most importantly the descent of humans, could be seen as the result of a simple physical process with no Creator involved. Many scientists have used this observation to argue for a totally atheistic view of reality.

For example, as noted by William Provine, a biologist and historian of science:

> Modern Science directly implies that there are no inherent moral or ethical laws, no guiding principles for human society. We must conclude that when we die, we die, and that is the end of us... Finally, free will as it is traditionally conceived simply does not exist. There is no way that the evolutionary process as currently conceived can produce a being that is truly free to make moral choices...[76]

The theologian John Haught called this train of thought *evolutionary materialism,*[77] which clearly is a subset of materialism. This is the milieu under which many scientists operate, although few of them are as strident as Provine, Richard Dawkins (see the Dawkins' quote in Chapter 2), and E.O. Wilson (see Wilson's quote at the beginning of Chapter 3).

Does the operation of natural selection during evolution

necessarily mean that religion is utterly irrelevant to modern man? Although many scientists obviously think so, Darwin did not. He was not solidly atheistic, as indicated by the last sentence in *The Origin of the Species*:

> There is grandeur in this view of life; with its several powers having been originally breathed by the Creator into a few forms or into one; and that, whilst this planet has gone cycling on according to the fixed law of gravity, from so simple a beginning endless forms, most wonderful and most beautiful have been, are being evolved.

Darwin may have added that quote as a way to mollify the religious critics to his theories[78], but several recent books also argue that accepting evolution via natural selection in no way necessitates the acceptance of atheism.[79]

Of course the authors writing books on the relation between science and religion are correct in pointing out that Darwinism is consistent with all but the narrowest interpretation of Christian theology, but unfortunately they tiptoe around the heart of the problem. They don't address how science views consciousness. As I noted in the previous chapter, those scientists who treat consciousness as merely chemical reactions in the brain are tacitly, if not blatantly, making a materialist declaration about the nature of reality. As such, they tend to confuse the statements that science can say with authority and those that are assertions of belief that cannot be tested by any scientific experiments. The statement that the Earth is 4560 million years old is a valid scientific statement because it deals with facts that anyone interested in the problem can objectively verify. Provine's statement that evolution implies there are no moral rules in human society is not a valid scientific statement because it deals with subjective values that lie well outside the purview of science.

Teilhardism

The great evolution debate involves two conflicting interpretations of how life arose on this planet. Materialists contend that life evolved as the result of a random process that is entirely mechanistic. Creationists and advocates of Intelligent Design believe that an unseen Creator (or an unspecified Intelligent Designer) created life and that evolution has not occurred at all, or at best has played a minor role in altering the products of creation. Within this debate, seldom is it mentioned that a third view exists. This interpretation, which was formulated by Pierre Teilhard de Chardin (1881-1955) following the philosophical writing Henri Bergson (1859-1941), postulates that evolution was not simply a mechanistic process, but that it involved spiritual aspects as well. Because Teilhard was the first modern scientist to present an explanation for evolution that seriously attempted to integrate the fields of science and religion into a coherent worldview, I call this view of evolution *Teilhardism*[80].

Henri Bergson

Bergson published his views of evolution in his book *L'Evolution créatrice* in 1907 (the English version, *Creative Evolution* appeared in 1911). In this book, he pointed out that life differs substantially from matter in that life is anti-entropic. By this he meant that all dead matter is subject to breakdown, decay, or erosion, whereas life involves growth and development. It is only after a creature dies that the material it amassed during its life begins to decay like any other dead matter. Bergson maintained that the vital force (élan de vital) that allows each individual being to grow and survive against the forces of decay is also the driving force in evolution. In Bergson's words:

> …life is like a current passing from germ to germ through the medium of a developed organism.

Bergson maintains that when this current comes upon obstacles from the external environment, it alters its form to overcome the obstacle and, in doing so, gives rise to evolution. To Bergson, evolution is a process of creativity, as he says:

> We claim...that the spontaneity of life is manifested by a continual creation of new forms succeeding others.

He contends that the vital force, which is the driving force for this creativity, appears in our minds as consciousness and more particularly as intuition. Hence, it is none other than the force that produces creativity in humans.

Materialists say that there are two big weaknesses to Bergson's view of evolution. Firstly, they contend that the concept of vitalism, which is central to the theory, is not needed to describe life. To materialists, the vitality of life is nothing other than an emergent property that appears once a certain critical state of complexity has been reached. This emergent property drives the metabolism of an organism and continues to do so until the parts of the organism begin to wear out, at which point the organism dies. The arguments materialists make against vitalism are not particularly persuasive. First off, simply dropping the name 'vital force' and calling it some unspecified 'emergent property' doesn't make the mystery of life go away, although it does, apparently give materialists an excuse to ignore it. Secondly, although materialists are not inclined to admit it, there is ample evidence supporting the existence of a vital force. For example, the concept of a vital force is inherent to Asian societies where it is called *qi* (in Chinese), *prana* (in Sanskrit) and *lung* (in Tibetan). In these societies various techniques, for example acupuncture, karate, and yoga, use this energy to induce healing and to provide power and vitality. Buddhism also recognizes a transcendent energy they call *prajna,* which is said to be the source of intuition and creativity, and they have developed many meditative techniques that allow a person to experience this energy.

The second and most critical problem of Bergson's view of evolution is that he is exceedingly vague about the processes by which 'creative evolution' proceeds. Although he speaks in length about the causes of evolution, he says little, apart from his support of Lamarckism, about how the process occurs. Lamarckism is a theory of evolution proposed by Jean Baptiste Lamarck (1744-1829) who theorized that the pressures within the environment induce evolutionary changes. According to Lamarck, if a member of a species develops a trait in response to environmental pressure, this trait will be passed on to the offspring. A corollary of Lamarckism is that changes in the environment will *cause* evolution. Place a population of animals in a cold climate and the climate will cause the succeeding generations to become increasingly accommodated to the cold. This is in contrast to Darwinism, which maintains that traits are developed by chance and those beings whose traits fit the surrounding environment best will have an edge in survival. Lamarckism has long gone out of favor in biology; more than a century of research has clearly shown that traits acquired during the lifetime of a parent are not passed on to the offspring.

Pierre Teilhard de Chardin

Teilhard, a Jesuit priest, was a paleontologist who made studies on the origin of human beings. Building on Bergson's concepts, he developed a theory of evolution that accommodated both his scientific knowledge and his deep religious faith. Teilhard developed his theory in the late 1930s, but his superiors within the Catholic Church were so disturbed by the theological implications of his theory they denied him the right to teach in France. They essentially exiled him from France for the last decades of his life, and prohibited him from publishing his theory during his lifetime. As a result, his book outlining the theory, *The*

Phenomenon of Man, wasn't published until 1955; the English version appeared in 1959.

In *The Phenomenon of Man* Teilhard maintained that evolution is not merely a theory, but rather that it is the most important force in the universe. As he said:

> Is evolution a theory, a system, or a hypothesis? It is much more: It is a general condition to which all theories, all hypotheses, all systems must bow and which they must satisfy... if they are to be thinkable and true. Evolution is a light illuminating all facts, a curve that all lines must follow.

To Teilhard, evolution is much more than biological evolution; it also includes processes by which the stars, the elements, and the Earth formed. By this definition, Teilhard notes that evolution has proceeded in three great waves: Firstly, evolution in the physiochemical realm produced what he calls the geosphere, then biological evolution produced the biosphere, and finally evolution of human culture produced what he called the noosphere. In this view, evolution isn't restricted to biological organisms; it also affects the material and cultural world. This is a prescient concept because Teilhard wrote his book long before most of our modern knowledge of Earth's evolution had developed. Modern theories describing the Big Bang, the formation of the heavier elements within the stars, the development of our solar system, and the way that primitive life produced the oxygenated atmosphere of today, were all unknown at the time Teilhard wrote *The Phenomenon of Man.* All those processes, however, can clearly be considered parts of Theilhard's physiochemical evolution, just as our relatively recent discovery of them can be considered part of the evolution of the noosphere.

One of the key concepts in Teilhard's theory is that a transcendent consciousness plays an important role in evolution.

In addition to their outer manifestation, the 'without' as Teilhard called it, all beings have an inner manifestation, the 'within'. The 'within' is easily recognized in the self-consciousness of humans, and we can infer that the higher mammals also show some aspects of consciousness. Teilhard maintained that consciousness is present in all beings, though it may be nearly unrecognizable in the simplest life forms. Not only that, he contended that consciousness is present to some extent in all matter, even if it cannot be measured (see for example Figure 28B).

If transcendent consciousness exists, it must interact with our minds in some way. Teilhard called the agent of this interaction, which produces intuition and creativity, *spiritual energy*. With this in mind, Teilhard distinguished between two types of energy: radial energy, which is the energy of the 'without' of matter, and tangential energy, which is the energy of the 'within'. Radial energy is the energy we recognize in the material world, such as thermal energy, chemical energy, or kinetic energy. In contrast, tangential cannot be directly measured physically. It is the energy of the 'within' of matter, and it increases with the increasing complexity of life.

Teilhard's theory (i.e. 'Teilhardism') agrees with Darwinism in that natural selection plays a key role in evolution. Teilhard maintained, however, that in addition to natural selection, the presence of a surrounding field of consciousness might give an added, though subtle, direction to the path of evolution. As Teilhard says:

> It is really only through strokes of chance that life proceeds, but strokes of chance which are recognized and grasped – that is to say psychically selected.

In Teilhard's opinion, chance mutations may be the dominant process during evolution of rather primitive creatures (reticulate evolution, the large-sale exchange of genes by simple one-celled organisms, was unknown at the time he was writing). Teilhard maintained that the role of consciousness (or spiritual energy) in evolution is manifested by the way that the nervous system of vertebrates has become increasingly complex over time. He contended that this increasing complexity indicated that evolution has had a clear direction. He called this process of directed evolution *orthogenesis*.

One of the key aspects of Teilhardism is that evolution involves the crossing of thresholds. A threshold is crossed when a creature evolves the ability to occupy niches that were previously inaccessible. When this happens a myriad of species quickly develop that exploit these newly available niches. For example, when tetrapods first developed lungs, which allowed them to live out of water, a large variety of amphibians and then mammal-like reptiles and reptiles radiated onto the landscapes of the planet. Teilhard maintained that the appearance of mankind involves another threshold; a breakthrough into the world of self-consciousness. This threshold, however, is different from all other evolutionary breakthroughs, in that it completely changed the process by which evolution takes place.

When ancient humans moved into different environments, they responded by changing their culture rather than their genes. Today, humans use their intelligence to gain access to all of Earth's environments. We can fly without wings and we can explore the depths of the ocean without having fins and flippers. As a result of this breakthrough into the world of self-consciousness, evolution is now taking place in the plane of human culture rather than in the biological plane.

This evolution within our human consciousness is Teilhard's third big wave of evolution. Teilhard called this new sphere of evolution the *noosphere* (from *nous*, which is Greek for mind). When evolution crossed the threshold to self-consciousness, its whole pattern changed, and individual human beings became parts of a larger organism, just as several hundred million years ago individual cells grouped together to form the first multicellular organism. To Teilhard, all of the changes that have taken place in human history, the changes in the economic and political structure of society and changes in science and religion, are part of the same evolution that has produced the variety of species within the plant and animal realms.

One of the key points in Teilhardism is that the noosphere is still evolving toward a higher consciousness and that some time in the distant future our collective consciousness will converge onto a focus point that he called the *omega point*. According to his theory, at the Omega Point, evolution will cease and humanity will be united with the ultimate consciousness and will be freed from its material envelope.

Response to Teilhard's Theory

Although the publication of *The Phenomenon of Man* met with popular acclaim, it was greeted with considerable criticism from both from scientists and theologians.[81] The theologians criticized Teilhard because his worldview failed to provide any role for the concept of evil. A few scientists were favorably disposed toward the theory, most importantly Julian Huxley, who wrote the foreword to the English edition of Teilhard's book. However, most scientific reviews were scathing. Despite the theological and scientific skepticism, the book met with great popular support. The *Phenomenon of Man* is still in print and dozens of books about Teilhard de Chardin and his theory have been published in the fifty years since his death. Teilhard de Chardin societies have been formed in the United States, Great Britain, and France and a journal, *The Teilhard Review* was published between 1966 and 1994. Not only did Teilhard have enormous influence in uniting the spheres of science and religion, his contention that evolution is presently manifested by changes within human culture has become an important tenet in much of the New Age literature.

Despite Teilhard's popularity among the public and his acceptance by a few biologists, such as Julian Huxley and Edward Dodson, his concept of evolution has not made a dent in the scientific literature. Biological Abstracts reports 1418 papers referring to Darwin between the years of 1990 and 2008; only 6 referred to Teilhard. Five of those six references to Teilhard relate to his work in paleontology; only one is related to his theory of evolution.

Teilhardism has not prospered in the scientific community because there are many criticisms of the scientific aspects of the theory. The problems that scientists have found with Teilhardism include:

1) Teilhardism has strong touches of Lamarckism. As noted above, Lamarckism postulates changes in the environment will *cause* evolution. This is in contrast to Darwinism, which maintains that traits are developed by chance and those beings whose traits fit the surrounding environment best will have an edge in survival.

2) Most biologists working in evolution doubt the veracity of orthogenesis, i.e. that evolution is directed. Orthogenesis is based upon the assumption that evolution is progressive. Many biologists doubt that evolution involves progress and hence, dispute the presumption upon which orthogenesis is constructed. Even if one accepted the concept of progressive evolution, many evolutionary scientists maintain that orthogenesis isn't valid because they contend that evolution operates totally by chance. A good example is this quote from Nobel Prize winner Jacques Monod:

> Chance *alone* is the sole source of every innovation, of all creation in the biosphere. Pure chance, absolutely free but blind, at the very root of this stupendous edifice of evolution: this central concept of modern biology is no longer one among other possible or even conceivable hypotheses. It today is the *sole* conceivable hypothesis; the only one that squares with observed and tested facts.[82]

With this view, there is no indication that evolution is anything other than a random process.

3) Teilhardism is not scientific. Many aspects of the theory simply cannot be tested by any objective means. This includes the concept of radial versus tangential energy, the within of beings, and especially the contention that consciousness is present to some extent in all existence, even in non-living matter. Most importantly, the theory also includes the concept of an Omega Point, that there is a point of pure consciousness toward which evolution is directed.

To a certain extent, it is not surprising that Teilhard's theory has elicited such a negative reaction from scientists. Even scientists who are naturalists (as opposed to materialists) would maintain that science involves only objective knowledge. Teilhard's theory was an attempt to unify his mystical insights and scientific knowledge to produce a coherent story for the origin of human beings. The introduction of subjective knowledge into what is nominally considered an objective science is sure to upset most scientists working in the field.

In contrast, it should also not be surprising that many non-scientists are receptive to Teilhardism. Whereas a unity of objective and subjective knowledge may not be necessary in the more material sciences, it is critical to understanding biology. Most people sense that living beings, at least the more advanced ones, are conscious. A science that studies life, therefore, is hollow unless it can take consciousness into account. Because attempts by scientists to explain consciousness in a purely materialistic manner produce such a depressingly bleak view of the human condition, it is understandable why Teilhardism has struck a positive cord with many people in the humanities.

An Assessment of Teilhardism

Because Teilhardism is a theory that combines faith with science, we can recognize aspects of it that can be accepted at three different levels. Some aspects of Teilhardism are based upon objective facts and are clearly scientific theories. Others are quasi-objective, they can be supported by logical construction using objective facts, but they involve premises that are not purely objective. Finally, there are aspects of Teilhardism that are almost entirely faith-based and cannot be tested by any scientific experiment. Below, I review Teilhardism and note which areas require more than 'objective' facts for acceptance.

Objective aspects of Teilhardism

Teilhard's contention that evolution involves crossing of thresholds is one concept that can easily be defended with facts.[83] There are many good examples of this in the paleontological literature. One would be the radiation of amphibians, reptiles, and mammal-like reptiles once vertebrates evolved mechanisms to survive on land. Another example would be the proliferation of mammalian species once they were released from the domination of the dinosaurs. Of course, the most obvious threshold is the development of self-consciousness in humans.

Teilhard's concept of three great waves of evolution is another aspect that is supported by observations. We have seen in Part II how the first great wave in the early ages of this universe produced the stars, the elements, and the Earth on which we reside. We also saw how the second wave, biological evolution, cannot be separated from physical evolution, since life and the composition of the atmosphere evolved together. Finally, the third wave of cultural evolution is a logical consequence of the development of human self-consciousness. A skeptic may not wish to consider all these as part of the same process, but there is little doubt that each type of evolution has occurred. Even some ardently materialistic scientists ascribe all these changes to this great sweep of evolution.[84]

It is important to note that each of these waves of evolution involved the appearance of an emergent property. As I noted in Chapter 12, the appearance of these new properties meant that a different process controlled each wave. Physiochemical evolution involved simple physical or chemical processes. For example, nuclear reactions began in response to the collapse of a gas cloud under the pull of gravity or different minerals crystallized as the molten Earth cooled. Because physical laws, such as gravity, nuclear physics or thermodynamics, governed these processes, given a few input parameters, scientists can do a reasonably good job modeling what happened during the Big Bang or during the crystallization of the molten Earth, even though humans clearly were not around to witness these events.

When life appeared on Earth, it brought with it an entirely new mode of evolution. In addition to chemistry and physics, life involves another critical process, the transfer of information. As we have noted above, this information is transferred genetically and propagates through a population in a Darwinian manner. As living creatures evolve, they pass the information about their adaptations from one generation to another in their genes. Unlike physiochemical evolution, however, there is no theory available that will allow scientists to predict the paths that genetic evolution would follow. Thus, there is no way a biologist could have predicted in advance the pathways that Devonian fishes would have followed to form humans.

Regardless of whether you consider consciousness as something produced in the brain or something accessed by the brain, human self-consciousness appeared as another emergent property. When self-consciousness appeared, it introduced a whole new way of transferring information. Cultural change takes place by exchange of ideas, rather than genes. Unlike genetic changes, which take generations to progress, the ideas of a single person can propagate through a culture in lightning speed. As a result, cultural changes can sweep through a population at a rate that is orders of magnitude faster than physical changes produced by genetics. For example, Darwin's theory of evolution sped through scientific culture in a few years; but none of the people believing in Darwinism had to be a direct descendent of Darwin. Furthermore, cultural information can be transferred from one person to another at any time in their lives, not merely by reproduction. Thus, cultural evolution is more closely related to Lamarckism than to Darwinism.[85]

It is important to note that, although each wave of evolution involved a change in the dominant mechanism of evolution, the evolutionary mechanisms present in earlier waves still continued. For example, physiochemical changes of the atmosphere continued, even as biological evolution took over as the dominant processes during the second wave of evolution. Likewise, both Darwinian and physiochemical evolution have continued as cultural evolution has proceeded; witness how humans have changed the genetic make-up of domestic plants and animals and how we inadvertently have changed the composition of the atmosphere.

Quasi-objective aspects of Teilhardism

As I noted in the previous chapter, there is no objective way to determine whether consciousness is an emergent or a transcendent property. Traditional views of evolution *assume* that consciousness is emergent, but there is no *a priori* reason why one has to make this assumption. If, instead, we *assume* that consciousness is transcendent, as is implied in Teilhardism, then certain conclusions logically follow. I call these aspects quasi-objective because they follow only after one assumes the existence of a transcendent consciousness.

For example, if we accept the existence of a transcendent consciousness, then it is easy to argue that evolution is progressive. Progressive evolution is a controversial topic among evolutionary biologists. It is clear that over time species have become more complex and more diverse, the question is whether these changes constitute progress. The word 'progress' implies a process whereby value increases over time. There are many biologists, such as Richard Dawkins, the author of *The Selfish Gene,* who maintain that the only true value in biological organisms is the information tied up in their genes. To these scientists, consciousness is merely an epiphenomenon. Because it doesn't make much difference to a gene whether it inhabits a human or a paramecium, these scientists would maintain that evolution has been a random walk and has not involved any progress at all. To those who consider consciousness valuable, and particularly to those who posit the existence of a transcendent consciousness, the increase in consciousness that is evident in creatures over time represents an increase in value. In this view, evolution is progressive. As I noted above, to Teilhard this progress is marked by the increasing complexity of the neurological systems of vertebrates over time.

We have seen that natural selection has enabled life to populate an incredible number of niches on Earth. Another way of saying this is that natural selection has allowed life to efficiently exploit the wide variety of energy fields that it has encountered. Some of the energy fields life has dealt with on Earth include the gravitational field as well as ranges in acidity and alkalinity, temperature, water salinity, partial pressure of oxygen, and water activity (or humidity). In the process, life has evolved to thrive in waters that range from highly acidic to highly basic, temperatures that range from subfreezing to boiling, and redox conditions ranging from anoxic to oxygen-saturated.

If we accept the premise that consciousness is transcendent, then consciousness becomes just another field within which natural selection has operated. One would expect that, just as it did for all the other fields encountered by life, natural selection would have allowed living organisms to exploit as much of the field of consciousness as is accessible. It is obvious that an increase in awareness provides a creature with an evolutionary advantage. With a greater awareness of its environment, a creature has a better chance to obtain food, to avoid predators, and, if it reproduces sexually, to find a good mate. Because awareness will provide a creature with an evolutionary advantage, it is easy to see how the operation of natural selection could result in an increase in consciousness. In particular, we saw in Chapter 10 how the use of tools by the first *Homo habilis* may have enhanced the development of the human brain.

These arguments mean that a self-conscious being (i.e. something like us) could have developed by a purely Darwinian process. It also means that the rise of human beings need not be the product of blind luck as many biologists contend. Self-consciousness was a niche screaming to be filled and the concept of convergent evolution says that sooner or later evolution would have stumbled onto the path to fill it[86]. In a similar way, the ability to fly is an important ecological niche and first insects, and then reptiles (i.e. pterosaurs), birds, mammals (i.e. bats) and finally humans evolved ways to exploit it.

Faith-based aspects of Teilhardism

There are many aspects of Teilhardism that must be accepted on faith. One of these is the concept of orthogenesis, or directed evolution. Whether one accepts orthogenesis depends entirely on the nature of one's faith. I have argued above that self-conscious beings *could* have evolved through a Darwinian process as evolution exploited the field of consciousness without necessarily being *directed*. Such a theory could be acceptable to agnostics who are willing to swallow the possibility that a transcendent consciousness exists or to followers of religions, such as Buddhism, that call for an impersonal nature to Ultimate Reality.

Christians and others who believe in the personal nature of Ultimate Reality might consider the expansion of life into the field of consciousness as a product of orthogenesis. Two types of orthogenesis are possible. In 'passive' orthogenesis, God simply provided the environment and the field of consciousness necessary for the evolution of conscious beings and let natural selection do the rest. In 'active' orthogenesis, in addition to providing a field of consciousness, God produced or directed the genetic mutations that lead to evolution and hence to orthogenesis. This seems to be the kind of orthogenesis that was envisioned by Teilhard and Bergson. The model of God's participation in evolution presented by Goswami is certainly one of 'active' orthogenesis[87], whereas the models of Ken Miller, and Hugh Rolston clearly contain aspects of 'passive' orthogenesis.[88] It is not clearly stated by them whether they imply 'active' orthogenesis as well. The humility of God as postulated in the theology of John Haught would also fit passive orthogenesis[89]. Because we have no way to prove that orthogenesis (either 'passive' or 'active') has occurred, this is an aspect of Teilhardism that must be accepted on faith.

Another aspect of Teilhardism that is impossible to validate scientifically is the concept of the 'within'. Most of us are quite certain that we have a consciousness (though some, like Francis Crick, would say that it is simply a chemical or electrical reaction in our brains). Many of us would accept that all animals are to some extent conscious, though only dimly so for simple life forms. Most scientists would consider that Teilhard's contention that consciousness permeates inert matter is untestable. However, if we accept the concept that consciousness is transcendent (cf. Figure 28B), then it logically follows that some aspect of this transcendent consciousness must be present within the matter that it encompasses. Indeed, there are some physicists who maintain that the strange behavior of the quantum world is pointing to the imminence of consciousness within matter.[90]

Many scientists also look askance at Teilhard's concepts of radial versus tangential energy, mainly because tangential (or spiritual energy) cannot be measured. However, the concept of spiritual energy is well accepted in religions. In Christianity it is known as the *Holy Ghost* and it is considered the energy by which God communicates with human beings. The terms used to describe spiritual energy in Eastern religions are the same as those to describe vital energy, i.e. *qi, prana, lung,* and *prajna.* Many Eastern religions, such as Taoism, Hindu and Buddhist Tantra and Tibetan Shamanism use meditative techniques to experience and concentrate these energies to gain spiritual insight.

Religious thinkers would maintain that the argument that spiritual energy cannot be measured is simply false. The instrument that you use to measure it, however, is yourself. They contend that if you undergo the intense training in a spiritual discipline, the nature of spiritual energy will be manifest in your mind. The materialists who argue that spiritual energy doesn't exist are simply not willing to undergo the practices necessary to experience it. Spiritual energy thus becomes another of those concepts that can only be verified by performing the empirical experiment yourself, i.e. by engaging in contemplative practice.

The question of whether the Omega Point actually exists and whether mankind will dissolve into it when the ultimate goal of evolution is reached, is, of course, another concept that cannot be settled scientifically. Teilhard and others who have written about his theory maintain that the Omega Point fits well with Christian theology; however, it also has aspects quite similar to Eastern religions. Both Hinduism and Buddhism contend that each individual being is a manifestation of a mind-stream that undergoes a series of rebirths. Within each lifetime this being has an opportunity to grow spiritually by becoming less attached to the ego that resides in the material body and, in the process, more sensitive to the needs of others. When a being becomes sufficiently advanced spiritually, he or she dissolves into the Godhead after death and no longer needs to incarnate in a material body. Whether this can happen for the megabeing known as the noosphere is another point that we must accept on faith.[91]

These four aspects of Teilhardism (orthogenesis, the 'within', radial vs. tangential energy, and the Omega Point) cannot be determined experimentally. Rather, they are all aspects of the theory that require contemplative practices or faith for acceptance. They give Teilhard's theory its depth and power, but really cannot be included within a scientific theory. Setting aside these faith-based aspects, Teilhardism is characterized by several aspects. These include:

1) Evolution involves three great waves, only one of which involved biological evolution and the last of which involves evolution in the cultural realm.
2) Evolution involves conquering of thresholds; the most recent of which is the development of self-consciousness in humans.
3) A transcendent consciousness is involved in evolution, if only as a passive potential field.
4) Evolution is progressive in that it involves the progressive opening of beings to consciousness.
5) Evolution has meaning. It is not a blind mechanistic process, but because it involves an opening of beings to the transcendent consciousness, it has profound meaning.

These points (especially the last three) set Teilhardism apart from evolutionary materialism.

A Comparison between Teilhardism and Intelligent Design

Because Teilhardism holds the possibility that evolution occurred through active orthogenesis, some would say that Teilhardism is a form of Intelligent Design. This is only true if one defines

Intelligent Design in its broadest form, namely that evolution has involved something more than a simple mechanistic process. It is not the kind of Intelligent Design (ID) defined by the movement that is trying to introduce ID into the science curriculum. There are three key points to this type of ID.

1) Life is simply too complex to have arisen by Darwinian processes and therefore some external intelligent designer must have caused the complexities we see in biological organisms today.
2) Evolution is simply a scientific theory and, because of this, ID, which is also a scientific theory, should be taught parallel with it in schools.
3) ID is a valid field of science that involves attempts to detect design in biology.

Teilhardism would not fit in to any three points of ID raised above. Like evolutionary materialism, Teilhardism is constructed on the scientific evidence for evolution; as a result, it does not require the argument of *irreducible complexity* to be valid. The concept of irreducible complexity was introduced by Michael Behe.[92] He noted that most biological processes and organs involve many complex parts and if you remove one part from an organ it becomes biologically useless. Behe notes that natural selection can only work with portions of organisms that are already working. Thus, he argues, evolution by natural selection could not build complex organs, biogeochemical processes, or a different species, because, some place along the way a mutation would have arisen with an organ that is half-way built. Such a mutation would be totally useless, would provide no adaptive benefit, and would not be preserved in the gene pool. As a result, Behe maintains that evolution cannot produce anything new and new forms must be derived from an Intelligent Designer.

This argument is flawed because evolutionary biology has

long known that a supposedly irreducibly complex organism could have evolved from pre-existing bits and pieces that played different, but still useful, functions in precursor organism. Thus, evolution doesn't involve producing entirely new structures from scratch, but rather subtle redesigning of pre-existing structures. A good example of this, as discussed in Chapter 10, is the way that organelles within eukaryotes may have formed by incorporation of various types of prokaryotes within a single cell.

In contrast to the proponents of ID, Teilhardism maintains that the paleontological evidence for the evolution of life is a fact, not an unproven theory. In fact, as noted above, Teilhardism defines evolution in much broader terms than do most biologists. In Teilhardism the physiochemical development of the universe, solar system, and Earth, as well as the development of culture are all part of evolution. It is true the Teilhardism questions the interpretation of evolution put forth by evolutionary materialism, but in doing so Teilhardism questions HOW evolution happened, not the fact that it happened. Although Teilhardism postulates that a transcendent consciousness may have been involved in evolution, if it was involved, it must have operated entirely within the frame of evolution that has been established from scientific data.

Unlike ID, Teilhardism does not consider the participation of a transcendent consciousness in evolution to be scientifically testable. When the advocates of ID define themselves as a scientific discipline, they make two mistakes. Firstly, they mistake objective knowledge, i.e. that of science, with subjective knowledge of faith. In Teilhardism, a transcendent consciousness could be involved in evolution as a passive field into which evolution expanded or it could take an active role in what I call *active orthogenesis*. I noted that there is no *objective* way to determine the difference between these two possibilities; this can only be affirmed by faith. Similarly, advocating the role of an Intelligent Designer in nature is faith-based (i.e. it involves subjective knowledge) and can never be proven objectively.

The third mistake the ID movement makes occurs when they define themselves as the 'science of design detection'. This definition entirely misrepresents how science operates. There is no way that ID can become a scientific discipline because it is not falsifiable. What the advocates of ID are doing is trying to use 'objective' data to prove a postulate, namely that natural features have been 'designed' by an intelligent force. As noted in Chapter 4, this is not how science operates. Science gathers data, postulates theories, and tries to *disprove* them. It never starts with a theory (i.e. that nature has been designed) and tries to *prove* it.

Teilhardism and Evolutionary Materialism

Most scientists would dismiss Teilhardism outright because it posits the existence of a transcendent consciousness and because certain aspects of it are faith-based, most importantly orthogenesis. They would say that the randomness of the mutations that produce evolution is good scientific proof against orthogenesis, be it 'passive' or 'active' (see the quote at the beginning of this chapter by Monod). Unfortunately, because evolution has operated over vast amounts of time, the hypothesis of 'randomness' upon which much of evolutionary biology is constructed is unfalsifiable. Experimental tests for randomness using complex organisms, whose generations last months or years, would take lifetimes. A number of creative experiments have, however, been run to see how populations of fast-reproducing bacteria or fruit flies adjust to changing conditions. These experiments show that populations tend to converge on one or more stable end points, a clear sign of adaptation. If evolution were totally random, then different populations would have evolved in different directions. It is true that the individual changes involved in this evolution could have arisen randomly, but the evolution itself clearly was adaptive.[93]

Most scientists would contend that 'consciousness has

transcendent aspects' or 'God has directed evolution' are statements of belief that cannot be scientifically tested. However, they do not recognize that similar statements inherent to evolutionary materialism, such as 'evolution is entirely a mechanistic process' or 'Chance *alone* is the sole source of...all creation in the biosphere.' are also statements of belief because they too cannot be tested.

Thus, both evolutionary materialism and Teilhardism agree with the objective facts of evolution and differ only on the subjective lenses through which they view these facts. Darwinism or natural selection is a valid process common to both these theories. In Figure 29 I show evolutionary materialism as being only an aspect of materialism because there are also arguments for materialism, such as the concept that consciousness is simply electrical reactions in your brain, that are not necessarily built upon natural selection. Teilhardism, in contrast, is an aspect of mysticism. I call the encompassing worldview of Teilhardism *mysticism,* rather than *religion* for three reasons. Firstly, I do this to acknowledge the mystical roots of Teilhard's theory, which all commentators on his theory recognize. Secondly, and more importantly, I do it to affirm that Teilhardism can only be tied to a religious view of the world if one recognizes religion as an expression of *mythos*. If we limit our view to the *logos* of religions, then clearly no such connection can be made. Finally, I consider it a portion of mysticism because only by obtaining a mystical sense of unity between objective and subjective reality can one really understand the world.

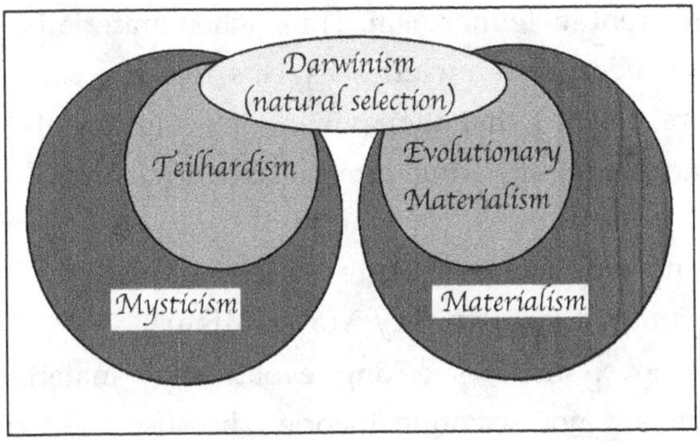

Figure 29 Diagram showing the relations between Darwinism, Teilhardism, and Evolutionary Materialism.

Because *both* theories fit all the data we have on the evolution of life, it is impossible to establish scientifically which of these two theories (evolutionary materialism or Teilhardism) is correct. The major difference between them is the role of consciousness, and, of course, consciousness is something that objective science can say virtually nothing about. What this means is that strictly speaking, *neither evolutionary materialism nor Teilhardism are scientific theories*. As we noted in Chapter 4, scientific theories must be falsifiable through experiments. However, we have seen that there is no experiment we can design that allows us to determine whether a transcendent consciousness permeates evolution. That we cannot do this is not particularly surprising. It is merely a manifestation of the fact that, when one is dealing with biological processes, a purely objective knowledge must fall short because, in addition to the outer aspects of creatures, one must consider the inner aspects, consciousness, as well. To *assume* that beings have no consciousness (which is inherent in evolutionary materialism) involves a premise that need not be valid. Indeed, materialists make other assumptions, such as that evolution proceeds only by chance, that cannot be scientifically validated. As such, evolutionary materialism carries a metaphysical implication that is similar to the aspects of faith that are inherent in Teilhardism. Thus, when materialists dismiss Teilhardism because it includes aspects that are not scientific, they ignore the fact that their views of evolution also include beliefs that, strictly speaking, are not scientific either.

Is there any way to Determine which is Valid: Teilhardism or Evolutionary Materialism?

As noted above, strictly speaking, evolutionary materialism and Teilhardism are not scientific theories, because they cannot be disproved. Rather, we must consider them as *metaphysical paradigms,* and we must look at evidence other than scientific data to determine which paradigm is valid. I have noted above that evolutionary materialism does a very bad job in explaining the nature of consciousness, the cause of creativity, or what happens at death. To the religiously inclined, these problems suggest that evolutionary materialism has critical weaknesses. Unfortunately, most materialists see no problem with these apparent weaknesses. After all, to them, consciousness is simply chemical reactions in your brain, creativity is simply the appearance of ideas in your head, and your consciousness simply gets switched off when you die.

There are two arguments against evolutionary materialism, however, that even atheists must admit to. First, the vast majority of Americans simply do not believe the mechanistic view of life put forth by most modern biologists. Second, ascribing natural selection to the formation of culture and religion produces many logical inconsistencies and simply doesn't work.

1) There is no popular acceptance of materialism. Although many scientists are completely convinced that materialism explains the phenomenal world, the vast majority of Americans believe otherwise. Ordinarily, scientists should not be concerned if the general public doesn't accept their theories because a substantial amount of prior education is commonly required before one can evaluate the veracity of most scientific theories. For example, only a small number of people have the mathematical background necessary to evaluate the subtleties of the quantum theory. Unlike the quantum theory, however, Darwin's theory of evolution is simple enough to be understood by grade-school students. This, of course, is one of the reasons why Creationists are so opposed to it. Even E.O Wilson, the founder of Sociobiology and an ardent materialist acknowledges in his book, *Consilience,* that the majority of Americans are reluctant to accept the concept of evolution. He notes:

> Transcendentalism, especially when reinforced by religious faith, is psychically full and rich; it feels somehow *right.* In comparison empiricism seems sterile and inadequate. In the quest for ultimate meaning, the transcendentalist route is much easier to follow. That is why, even as empiricism is winning the mind transcendentalism is wining the heart.[94]

Wilson has an easy way to explain why materialism (or empiricism as he calls it) is not popular with the American public.

> The human mind evolved to believe in the gods. It did not evolve to believe in biology.

Wilson is implying two things here (and in the quote from his book that I gave at the beginning to Chapter 3). One is that the religious experience has evolved genetically to control the way humans behave. The other is that the majority of the American people, unlike Wilson and his fellow materialists, are still primitive, wrong-thinking beings who are incapable of seeing through their genetic make up and hence cannot think clearly. This reasoning is insidious for two reasons. Firstly, it belittles any intellectual arguments made by the opponents to evolutionary materialism. Secondly, it insulates the materialists from any cogent arguments about the weaknesses of their theories.

Unlike evolutionary materialism, Teilhardism has an easy explanation for why so many people don't believe in the type of evolution described by the materialists. Simply put, most people have had some experience of the transcendent nature of consciousness postulated by Teilhardism. As a result, they do not accept the mechanistic view of biology simply because it belies their direct experience of a spiritual aspect to the world.

2) Darwinism does a very poor job explaining the origin of religion and human culture. The attempts materialists make to explain the evolution of human culture using natural selection result in a tangle of logical inconsistencies.[95] It is true that cultures which have come up with powerful inventions have been successful in a way that is similar to natural selection. However, the functional view that those cultures came up with the inventions as a way to become successful is woefully oversimplified, particularly when applied to religion. Over the past decade a lot of books have been written using 'scientific' techniques to explain how cultures arose. Many of these studies have been devoted to the origin of religion, which is a totally mysterious phenomenon to someone of materialistic bent. The following six theories have arisen that attempt to describe how religion appeared in the human culture (it should be noted that the proponents of any one of these theories are often dismissive of the others).

1. Because humans have such a long childhood, children have evolved to depend on their parents. Religion evolved as a cultural manifestation of this dependence (i.e. God is a big daddy.)[96]
2. Shamanistic healing was the only healing available to primitive humans and, according to the proponents of this model, shamanistic healing worked because it hypnotized people into feeling that they were cured. Because those people who were easily hypnotized had a better rate of survival, a gene evolved that allowed people to be hypno-

tized by shamans. This 'hypnotisability' center in the brain became the God-center.[97]

3. Organized religion formed from folk religion when the tribal bosses used it to gain power over the masses – i.e. the bosses became appointed (or anointed) by the gods. According to this theory, religion formed as an act of coercion.[98]
4. Organized religion arose through group selection – those folks who had the religion that most advocated cooperation became more prosperous (and successful) than those who did not.[99]
5. Religion is simply a market decision; people buy into a religion because they get from it what they cannot get otherwise, immortality.[100]
6. Religion is a mental virus that captures people's minds and makes them servants that further propagate this virus.[101]

All of these theories suffer from one critical problem. They insist on studying the objective aspects of religion without touching the subjective experience. Since, as we noted in the very beginning of this book, the religious experience is highly subjective, studying religion from a scientific (i.e. objective) starting point entirely misses the internal experience that makes religions so vibrant and vital.

In a way, a materialist making a 'scientific' study of religion is akin to a blind person writing a history of art. It is certainly possible for a blind person to write about art history; he (or she) could rely upon contemporary commentaries as the basis of this history. However, this person would have no experience of how the nature of light is transmitted in the Impressionist paintings, of the garish color of Van Gogh, or of how the Cubists attempted to show subjects from all view points at once. As a result, although a blind person might be able to write a history of art that could appear reasonable to another blind person, it is likely to have some glaring errors that are obvious to those who can actually see the art that the author is writing about.

To understand how the 'scientific' study of religion is inherently flawed, consider what scientists from an alien planet would think as they analyzed human culture. They might come up with the same theories to explain religion as those outlined above. Wouldn't they also be intrigued by the evolution of science? They obviously would have observed that modern industrial society had evolved alongside modern science. Wouldn't this lead to a functionalist view of science? The aliens might consider that physics evolved to provide the machines necessary for modern life, chemistry evolved to produce the many complex chemicals a modern society needs, and geology evolved to provide the natural resources necessary to produce the machines and to obtain the fuels necessary to run them. These alien theorists, however, would have as tough a time understanding the development of 'curiosity-driven' science as did the officials in the Reagan administration who coined that term to disparage research that had no immediate monetary gain. Why would a scientist spend his whole life studying ants (as did E.O Wilson) when all one needs to get rid of them is a little well-applied insecticide? Why would a scientist spend his life studying snails on a desert island (as did J. Steven Gould) when there is no obvious economic gain?

Scientists who study the evolution of culture don't have a functionalist view of science, nor do they worry about the origin of 'curiosity-driven' science because they are immersed in the world of science. They know the thrill of discovery that makes 'curiosity-driven' science so appealing so they never bother to wonder how science evolved. However, the religious experience is completely alien to them. In none of the scientific studies of religion do the authors mention the experiences described by Thomas Keating and the Snowmass group that is referred to in Chapter 5. They avoid mentioning the religious experience for two important reasons. Firstly, these authors are wedded to the belief that only objective knowledge is important, therefore they believe that they need not concern themselves about the subjective experience of religious believers (despite the fact that they are well aware of how their subjective experiences drive their interest in science). Second, and perhaps more important, if they acknowledged the validity of the religious experience, they would have to admit to the possibility that the experience may be more than simply an epiphenomenon of the mind.

There is another good reason why Darwinist models fail when applied to the evolution of culture. In a way very similar to the mistakes made by the Creationists, materialists confuse objective with subjective knowledge. They err in assuming that the processes that occur in the material world (i.e. that of animals) can be applied to the subjective world (i.e., the world of ideas). Although Darwinism adequately describes the process of biological evolution, it is not valid to use it as a way to describe the evolution of human culture. The cultural aspects of humanity, such as science, ethics, and religion are almost entirely subjective in nature, and, as we noted in Chapter 3, it is not valid to apply theories designed to describe the objective observations of science to the subjective world of human behavior.

It is much easier to understand the origin of religion if one accepts Teilhardism. If evolution has involved progressive opening to a transcendent consciousness, as Teilhardism maintains, then those aspects of human behavior that arise from interaction with Ultimate Reality, such as cooperation, altruism, and generosity, are parts of the human inheritance. There is no need to come up with convoluted 'biological' explanations for those aspects of human behavior that do not 'fit' the materialist image that beings are driven entirely by self-interest.[102] Teilhardism maintains that religion arose as a way to provide humans access to the transcendental aspects of consciousness, not simply as a way to enhance the survival of a clan or group or, what's worse, by mistake.

Chapter 14
Future of the Debate

As the arguments above show, the Creationists and their allies are not merely a few extremists who are fighting a rear-guard battle against the inevitable march of science. Rather, the Creationism and Intelligent Design movement is a response to the cold, mechanistic worldview of evolutionary materialism. The great debate between evolution and Creationism is therefore not a lingering remnant of the great dispute between Galileo and the Church, as many scientists view it. Rather, it is a manifestation of a major weakness that is inherent to the materialistic view of evolution presented by most scientists. Because of this, the debate is not likely to dissipate quietly, as many scientists maintain, once the Creationists finally recognize the failing of their ways and gracefully retire from the field of combat. It is a fair question to ask, therefore, how this dispute, which has rankled the American body politic for more than 80 years, can finally be settled.

Although predictions of the future are frequently wrong, several points are obvious. Both sides are well entrenched and have been arguing the same points for over a century. Clearly the controversy will not disappear as long as the materialists and Creationists maintain mutually antagonistic views. As noted above, the Creationists are not likely to change their views, because if they do so, they will automatically admit defeat. Change, however, is a characteristic of science. Is it possible that the scientific view of evolution may change sufficiently so that it is no longer seen to be a threat by Fundamentalist Christians?

Although evolutionary materialism is clearly the dominant paradigm in the biological sciences today, as we noted in the previous chapters, when it deals with the evolution of non-material aspects of humanity, such as culture and religion, it is clearly ridden with inconsistencies. The convoluted explanations required for evolutionary materialism to explain the origin of culture and religion make it look like a dying paradigm. In ways it appears similar to Ptolemy's theory, which required wheels upon wheels to explain the movement of the planets in a geocentric solar system. Ptolemy's theory, of course, lasted for two thousand years before its inconsistencies brought it down. The important question determining the future of the great evolution debate, therefore, is whether evolutionary materialism will remain the dominant paradigm for scientists or whether it will be replaced by a paradigm similar to Teilhardism that can accommodate a transcendent consciousness. Today, Teilhardism is hardly mentioned in academia (except perhaps in the fields of philosophy or theology); however, this does not mean that Teilhardism is dead. Evolutionary materialism is the child of materialism and as such, its fate as the dominant paradigm for biological science strongly depends on how well materialism retains its hold on Western culture.

As noted in Chapter 2, materialism took over as the dominant worldview of Western society in the 19th century. One of the key concepts of 19th century science was the assumption that the nature of the objective world 'out there' is independent of the observer. This concept worked very well in the world of Newtonian physics where the behavior of objects could be described by inviolate laws. However, in the early decades of the 20th century, this idea that science deals with an objective world independent of the mind of the observer began to crumble.

A minor problem in physics at the end of the 19th century was the question of why light emitted from a hot object changes its color as the temperature of that object increases. We all know that 'white hot' is hotter than 'red hot', but what controls the wavelength of this emitted light? In 1900 a German physicist, Max Planck, produced a neat mathematical equation that solved this problem. To construct his equation he had to assuming that light was emitted as little packets that he termed quanta. At first, these quanta were considered simply a mathematical convenience, but a few years later Albert Einstein showed that the energy of electrons emitted when light impacts on a metal surface are also quantized, just like the light that is hitting the surface. This means that a quantum of light, which we now call a photon, is a real object, not just a mathematical construct. This presented physicists with a paradox, because they already knew that light behaves like a wave. Light diffracts like a wave and different wavelengths of light have different colors. How then could light be a particle and a wave at the same time?

This paradox became worse as physicists probed the nature of the atom in the early decades of the 20th century. The first model of the atom, which was presented by Neils Bohr, held that the atom was constructed like a tiny solar system in which electrons, like little planets, revolved around the protons and neutrons, which are clustered together in the middle of the atom like a tiny sun. Electrons are emitted from an element in quanta because they occupy fixed orbitals around the nucleus. Each orbital has different energy so that when an electron 'jumps' from one orbital to another a fixed amount of energy is emitted or absorbed.

This 'solar system' view is still the common picture of atoms that you see in advertisements or company logos, but it has long since been dropped from the world of physics. In the early 1920s a French physicist, Louis de Broglie, put forth in his Ph.D. thesis that electrons, like light, could be described as waves. The Swiss physicist Erwin Schrödinger took this concept and developed the science of wave mechanics. In 1925 he showed that electrons are fixed to given 'orbitals' within an atom because those are the energy values where the electron has an integer number of waves.

Because electrons had originally been defined as units of

electrical current, scientists obviously viewed them as particles. Now, suddenly, electrons were shown to behave as if they were waves. How was it that electrons and light were able to behave both like a wave and like a particle? Physicists quickly found that the kind of behavior displayed by electrons or photons depends on the way they are observed. If you set up an experiment to measure the diffraction of light or electrons, you will see both of them behaving as waves. If you set up an experiment to measure their energy, you would see them as particles. This was the first finding of quantum physics that began to unravel the solid materialistic basis of science that was inherited from the 19th century.

Another impact of the quantum theory was that it destroyed, at the subatomic scale at least, the concept in classical physics that, given the right equations and the right experiments, scientists could predict *everything* about the world. Werner Heisenberg was the first to address this problem in 1927 when he postulated his famous uncertainty principle. He noted that it is impossible for scientists to know both the momentum and the position of an electron with accuracy. Experiments designed to determine the location of an electron will necessarily affect its momentum, and those designed to measure its momentum will affect its position.

A third problem introduced by quantum theory is that it brings the concept of probability into the physical world. Probability is fine when you want to calculate the likelihood that you will get heads five times in a row when you flip a coin. However, many scientists found it distressing to discover that processes of the sub-microscopic world could only be described with probability functions. For example, we all know that the element radium is radioactive. This radioactivity is produced by the breakdown of a radium atom to a daughter product and a released particle. Physicists can predict exactly how many radioactive particles will be emitted from a given mass of radium over a given period. However, they cannot predict which atom of radium will breakdown at any particular time. No amount of data a scientist can collect will give that information. This means that there is an inherent unknowability to the sub-atomic world.

These questions about reality that the quantum theory has thrust upon us have produced many popular books that relate quantum physics to mysticism.[103] Although it is popular, 'quantum mysticism' is criticized by both scientists and philosophers for misinterpreting both physics and mysticism.[104] Irrespective of whether quantum physics carries any mystical implications, it has effectively destroyed the assumptions inherent in Newtonian physics that there is an objective reality 'out there' and that science merely involves recording events that occur in that reality. The advent of the quantum theory has eroded the barrier between the observed and the observer to the extent that, in the world of elementary particles at least, the nature of the universe can no longer be considered independent of the mind of the observer. Even worse (for materialists at least), modern physics has shown that the material world doesn't really exist at all. If you look deeply enough into any chunk of matter, all you will find is energy. The material world has turned out to be exactly what the Hindu philosophers have always said that it is: maya, an illusion.

The changes that the quantum theory have brought to our understanding of the physical world over the past century have considerably weakened the materialistic view of the sub-atomic world. This weakening, however, hasn't propagated far into other fields of science. Because biology, for example, does not deal with processes that occur on the scale of electrons, it has been untouched by the revolution that quantum mechanics has thrust upon the physics community. This is not a situation, however, that can last for long. As physicists like to point out (often with a sense of snobbery), ultimately, all science is built upon physics. If materialism is losing its hold in the world of physics, it won't be long before its hold on the other fields of science will also slacken. After all, a philosophy built upon the premise that only the material world is real isn't very robust when science is increasingly telling us that, deep down, the material world is merely energy. In a way, we could say that the body of materialism is like an antebellum mansion that is infested by termites. Although its facade is ornate and elegant, the beams that hold up the building are completely rotten. Sooner or later a hurricane will come along that will reduce the mansion to rubble.

In addition to the development of the quantum theory, materialism is threatened by the spiritual awakening that has characterized the latter half of the 20th century. It is not clear whether this awakening has appeared as the direct result of the erosion of objectivism that quantum mechanics forced upon the science of physics or whether the timing is simply a coincidence. After all, as I noted earlier, the Scientific Revolution has enhanced the ability for people around the world to communicate. Not only has this changed the way that the world's economy and politics operate; it has also affected the sphere of religion. It has provided the opportunity, for the first time in history, for a close dialogue among the world's religions, and this is having a profound effect on how we will view religion in the 21st century.

The historian Arnold Toynbee once remarked that perhaps the most important development in the 20th century was the opening of communication between Christianity and Buddhism.[105] Apparently, Toynbee thought that if Christianity, which is a theistic religion, could find common ground with Buddhism, a non-theistic religion, there would be room for all religions to find commonality. This growing communication among religions has important implications for the future. As noted by the spiritual thinker Wyane Teasdale:

> We are at the dawn of a new consciousness, a radically fresh approach to our life as a human family in a fragile world. This birth into a new awareness, into a new set of historical circumstances, appears as a number of shifts in our understanding. Each of these shifts represents dramatic change; taken together they will define the thought and culture of the third millennium.... perhaps the best name for this segment of historical experience is the Interspirital Age.[106]

A good example of this change is the fact that in the dawning years of the 21th century, for the first time in history, a student could take instruction in the spiritual training of any religion, without first having to abandon his or her own religion.

Clearly, the unity of the world's religions cannot be realized if one holds to Fundamentalist beliefs. Under these beliefs, the Scriptures of the various religions are contradictory and there is no room for dialogue. It is only by reading those Scriptures as *mythos* that can one see that all religions arise from a common ineffable experience. The communication among religions, therefore, means that, at last, after almost five centuries in retreat, *mythos* is beginning to reassert itself in Western society.

The erosion of the materialistic view in the world of physics and the rediscovery of *mythos* in the world's religions could mark the beginning of a process that will eat away at the atheism that so dominates the worldview of science. To a large extent, atheism feeds off of Fundamentalism. When religion is presented in terms of *logos* alone it looks as if it is asking people to believe in fairy tales. This is one reason why so many people in academia today consider religion to be anti-intellectual. Atheists can easily dismiss the existence of a God who is seen as some old wise man living somewhere up in the sky, who knows everything, and who actually controls what happens in the world. Atheists also point out that it is very difficult to accept the conclusion that there is only one chosen religion and that the followers of all the other religions are bound to spend an eternity in Hell.

It is far more difficult for atheists to argue against the validity of religion when it is defined as faith in the existence of a transcendent consciousness. How can you dismiss the contention that this transcendent consciousness is accessible through practices such as meditation or contemplative prayer simply because you haven't had that experience yourself?[107] As *mythos* grows in acceptance, it will become increasingly easy for intellectually-oriented people to accept religion as a field worthy of study. Such study, however, will not involve memorizing the words in the holy texts. Rather it will involve contemplation so that the student gains access to the mystical experience upon which all religion is based. In other words, the study of religion will become more obviously experiential. The philosopher Ken Wilber maintains that this is one of the keys to uniting religion with science. Science is experiential knowledge gained in the objective realm, and Wilber maintains that using the same experiential approach to the subjective realm is the one way of healing this deep rift.[108]

If the spiritual awakening predicted by Teasdale does take hold in our society, contemplative practice with its inherent mystical insights will become a common part of all humanity's intellectual environment. This will have drastic effects on how we view science. Rather than being the only worthwhile intellectual endeavor for members of Western society (as implied in Wilson's quote at the beginning of Chapter 3), science will be only one of several ways we can view the world. This will have little impact on the operation of sciences that deal entirely with the material world, such as physics, chemistry, or geology. However, it will have dramatic impacts on biology and the other sciences that study living beings. Because living beings have some level of consciousness, in an interspiritual society, such as the one envisioned by Teasdale, science will not treat creatures simply as material objects; they must include some consideration of their consciousness. This will clearly affect how science views evolution. As we noted in Chapter 13, the only distinction between Evolutionary Materialism and Teilhardism is the contention that in the latter evolution involves a transcendent consciousness. As more biologists become aware that consciousness is transcendent, Teilhardism should become more widely accepted in the scientific community.

This leaves us with the interesting possibility that the spiritual awakening in Western society may produce a paradigm shift from evolutionary materialism to something similar to Teilhardism. Because the difference between the two paradigms is metaphysical, this paradigm shift, unlike most other scientific revolutions, will be driven by cultural changes, rather than by any new scientific discoveries. Evolutionary materialism is by far the major paradigm today (Figure 30), but as our society awakens from the long illusion of materialism, a view of evolution similar to Teilhardism may take over. I show the transition in Figure (30) with question marks for two reasons. Firstly, it is by no means certain that the subtle changes we see in society today will gather together into the massive spiritual awakening foreseen by Teasdale. Secondly, if it does happen, I have no idea whether the transition will happen in decades or centuries.

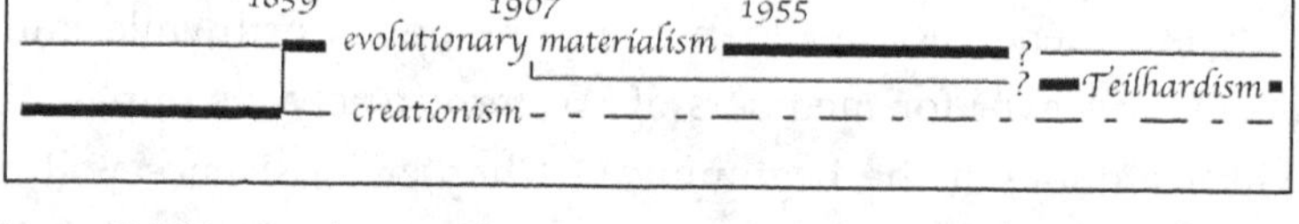

Figure 30 Diagram showing the possible paradigm changes on evolution from Creationism to Evolutionary Materialism to Teilhardism. 1859 = publication of *The Origin of The Species*, 1907 = publication of *Creative Evolution*, 1955 = publication of *The Phenomenon of Man*.

It is important to note that this proposed paradigm shift is in no way like the paradigm shift envisioned by the Intelligent Design Creationists. The Intelligent Designer Creationists aim to produce a paradigm shift that will replace 'atheist science' with 'theistic science'. Such a 'paradigm shift' is profoundly anti-scientific and could only be imposed from the outside. True paradigm shifts occur within science as a natural evolution of theories. If our society does become more spiritually inclined, which it appears to be doing, it will clearly affect how scientists view evolution, but it won't involve the total dropping of the scientific method, as advocated by the purveyors of theistic 'science'.

If this paradigm shift happens, the concept of evolution will no longer carry the implication of a spiritual vacuum, which it does in evolutionary materialism. Rather, it will become a key theory that ties the fields of science and religion together. This is one of the aspects of Teilhardism that has lead to its popularity among many humanists. Teilhardism allows room for a transcendent consciousness that seems to be lacking in many present versions of evolution. Thus, should Teilhardism become the major paradigm for evolution, a large part of the impetus that drives some Christians to question the validity of evolution will disappear.

Ironically, even if mainstream biology develops a paradigm that allows a role for transcendent consciousness in the evolution of life, it still will not terminate the great debate. This is because the Creationists, particularly the Young-Earth Creationists, are not likely to drop their fixation on a Biblical origin of the Earth. Young-Earth Creationists save their greatest vitriol for Christians who 'sell out' their religion by accepting evolution.[109] They certainly will still rail against any theory that doesn't ascribe to the Biblical age of the Earth.

Even though Creationism won't go away, the rise of Teilhardism will make it far more difficult for the Creationists to get their message across. Creationism and Intelligent Design currently resonate with the population because so many people have a sense of a spiritual presence in the world, a presence that is lacking in the present teachings on evolution. As long as science is disdainful of the possibility of a transcendent consciousness, Creationists have an easy time appealing to these people, even if they don't find all aspects of the Creationist credo particularly convincing. However, if Teilhardism becomes the major paradigm for evolution, then Creationism will no longer have a lock on religion. As a result, people who are in doubt as to which worldview is valid, particularly those who may have to make decisions regarding the teaching of evolution in schools, may be more sensitive to the many logical inconsistencies in both Creationism and Intelligent Design.

The advent of Teilhardism, therefore, should take much of the storm and fury out of the great debate. Because it shows how a transcendent consciousness can be accommodated within evolution, Teilhardism will weaken the arguments of both the materialists and the Creationists who maintain that Darwinism is equivalent to atheism. Thus, if Teilhardism does become an important paradigm for evolution, it will marginalize the views of those parties who hold the most extreme positions on evolution. If so, it is reasonable to expect that, even if the great debate doesn't disappear, it will fade from a controversy that resonates through America's whole political and social structure to a question that has relevance to only a few on the fringes of our society.

End Notes

[1]. See for instance Morris and Parker (1982) and Morris (1985).

[2]. These books include Ruse (1982), Futayama (1983), Scott and Cole (1985), Young (1985), and Berra (1990).

[3]. A few of these papers and books include Johnson (1991), Behe (1996), Dembski (1998, 2002), and Wells (2002).

[4]. For more details on the history of the Kansas School board's decisions on evolution see Miller (2008).

[5]. See for example Miller (1999, 2002), Pennock, (1999, 2002), and Scott (2002).

[6]. For a more detailed discussion of this see Pennock (1996).

[7]. See Larson and Witham (1997, 1998).

[8]. Dawkins (1995).

[9]. Crick (1997).

[10]. Provine (1988).

[11]. For a detailed discussion of this point see Armstrong (1993, 2000).

[12]. Plantinga (1991).

[13]. See Miller (1999), Van Till (1991), Clouser (1999), and Haught (2000).

[14]. See Raymo (1998) and Gould (1999).

[15]. See Gould (1999).

[16]. This term should not be mistaken for Logos, which, according to Christian theology, is the spirit of Christ as revealed in our ability to reason.

[17]. See Kuhn (1962).

[18]. It is only fair to note that under Pope John Paul the Catholic Church has explicitly accepted the validity of evolution, although recent edicts under Pope Benedict have softened this support significantly.

[19]. See Borgman (1998).

[20]. Quote from Greenburg (2000).

[21]. For example see, Harris (2004), Dawkins (2006), and Dennett (2006).

[22]. See Huxley (1943).

[23]. See for example Hixon (1978), Smith (1991), Teasdale (1999).

[24]. See Keating (1995), Teasdale, (1999).

[25]. See Hixon (1992).

[26]. Smith (1991).

[27]. DeMello (1990).

[28]. Merton (1972).

[29]. See Hixon (1978).

[30]. There are many particles that are more elementary than these, but these are elementary enough for our purposes.

[31]. For a good narration of how this problem was solved see Dalrymple (1991).

[32]. Data from Dalrymple (1991).

[33]. I will say more about the evolution of porpoises and their relatives in chapter 10.

[34]. See Morris (2003)

[35]. Modified after Wong et al, (2007)

[36]. Data from Delsemme (1998).

[37]. See Wills and Bada (2000).

[38]. Russell and Hall (1997).

[39]. Modified after Stetter (1998)..

[40]. See Kaufmann (1995).

[41]. For example see Johnson (1991) or Goswami (2008).

[42]. Data from Denison (1956).

[43]. Modified after Thewissen and Williams (2002).

[44]. This conclusion comes from the oxygen isotopic composition of the teeth of individuals in these families. The teeth from family 2 have compositions likely to reflect surface water; those from Family 3 have compositions closer to seawater (see Thewissen and Bajpail, 2001).

[45]. For details see Thewissen and Bajpail (2001).

[46]. Data from Berner & Canfield (1989), Holland (1994), Rye and

Holland (1998) and Beerling et al. (2002).

47. Over the past few years sophisticated instruments have been developed that can measure isotopic differences in metals that are present in sedimentary rocks only in very minute quantities. The isotopic composition of some metals, such as molybdenum and osmium, is sensitive to small changes in oxidation conditions. As a result, this new tool has spurred active research into how the Earth's atmosphere has changed over time. It is likely that within a decade or so geochemists will have characterized the changes in the oxygen content of the atmosphere and the sea floor through the Precambrian and into the Cambrian in great detail.

48. See Margulis (1970).

49. Johnson (1991).

50. See Towe (1970); Seilacher (1993), and Drury (1999).

51. See Towe (1970).

52. After Berner and Kothavala (2001).

53. Modified from Stringer (2003) and Asfaw et al. (2002).

54. After Kappelman (1996) and Ruff et al. (1997).

55. See Parker and Gibson (1979).

56. Gould (1999).

57. Ruse (2001) .

58. See Behe (1996).

59. See Kitchner (2001).

60. See for example Futuyma (1983) Berra (1990), Miller (1999) Pennock (1999), and Kitchner (2001).

61. For a good discussion of this see Smith (2001).

62. See Van Till (1991).

63. For a more detailed discussion of this see Pennock (1996) and Smith (2001).

64. Dennett (1991).

65. See Newberg, et al. (2001).

66. The concept of emergent properties was first introduced by Morgan (1927) and is a major topic of study in the modern

field of complexity.

67. Noelle (2003).

68. Russell (1961).

69. Wilber (1995).

70. See Moody (1975).

71. See Ellwood (2002).

72. See Kelley and Callanan (1992).

73. See Ray (2001).

74. See Blackman (1997).

75. See Ray (2001).

76. Provine (1988).

77. See Haught (2000).

78. See Birx (1990).

79. For example see Miller (1999), Gould (1999), Haught (2000), Ruse (2001), Dowd (2007), Gibberson (2008).

80. In my definition *Teilhardism* is a theory that posits the participation of a transcendent consciousness in evolution. The word does not refer in any way to the many theological writings of Teilhard, some of which still produce considerable debate (see Smith, 1988).

81. See Dodson (1984) for details on the response of the Biology community to Teilhard's book.

82. Monod (1972).

83. See Dodson (1984) for a good discussion of this.

84. See Chaisson (2001).

85. See Rolston (1999).

86. Similar arguments are raised by Morris (2003).

87. See Goswami (2008).

88. See Miller (1999) and Rolston (1999).

89. See Haught (2000).

90. For example see Kafatos and Nadeau (1990) and Goswami (1993).

91. It is Wilber's (2006) view that the evolution of the noosphere is not the same as personal evolution and that the Omega

Point is not likely to exist.

92. See Behe (1996).

93. For more on this see Travisano et al, 1995; and Morris (2003).

94. Wilson (1998).

95. See Rolston (1999).

96. See Dawkins (2006).

97. See McClenon (2002).

98. See Diamond (1997).

99. See Wilson (2002).

100. See Stark and Fink (2000).

101. See Dawkins (2006).

102. For a good introduction to this view see Richard Dawkins 1976 book *The Selfish Gene.*

103. The classic book of this type is Capra (1975) but others include Zukov (1975), Kafatos & Nadeau, (1990) and Goswami (1993).

104. For a discussion on the validity of the physics in quantum mysticism see Gell-Mann (1994); for a discussion on how it misinterprets mysticism see Jones (2008).

105. Quoted from Teasdale (1999).

106. Teasdale (1999).

107. Dawkins tries to make this argument in his 2006 book *The God Delusion,* by saying that such experiences are simply hallucinations, but he gives very little solid evidence to back up his contention.

108. See Wilber (1998).

109. As noted by Pennock (1999)

References

Armstrong, K., 1993, *The History of God. The 4000-year quest of Judaism, Christianity, and Islam.* New York, Ballantine Books.

Armstrong, K., 2000, *The Battle for God: Fundamentalism in Judaism, Christianity and Islam.* New York, Ballantine Books.

Asfaw, B., Gilbert, W.H., Beyene, Y., Hart, W.K., Renne, P.R., WoldeGabriel, G., Vrba, E.S., White, T.D., 2002, *Remains of Homo erectus from Bouri, Middle Awash, Ethiopia. Nature,* 416, 317-320.

Beerling, D.J., Lake, J.A., Berner, R.A., Hickey, L.J., Taylor, D.W., and Royer, D.L., 2002, Carbon isotope evidence implying high O_2/CO_2 ratios in the Permo-Carboniferous atmosphere. *Geochemica Consomchemia Acta,* 66, 3757-3767.

Behe, M.J., 1996, *Darwin's Black Box: The Biochemical Challenge to Evolution.* New York, The Free Press.

Berner, R.A. and Canfield, D., 1989, A new model for atmospheric oxygen over Phanerozoic time. *American Journal of Science,* 289, 333-361.

Berner R.A. and Kothavala, Z., 2001, GEOCARBIII: A revised model of atmospheric CO_2 over Phanerozoic time. *American Journal of Science,* 301, 182-204.

Berra, T.M., 1990, *Evolution and the Myth of Creationism.* Stanford, Stanford University Press.

Birx, H.J., 1990, *Interpreting Evolution (Darwin & Teilhard de Chardin).* Buffalo, NY Prometheus Press.

Blackman, S., 1997, *Graceful Exits. Death Stories of Tibetan, Hindu & Zen Masters,* New York, Weatherhill Press.

Borgman, L., 1998, The Zen of Research, *Journal of Geoscience Education,* 46, 346-353.

Capra, F., 1975, *Tao of Physics: An Exploration of the Parallels Between Modern Physics and Eastern Mysticism.* Berkeley Ca. Shambhala.

Chaisson, E.J., 2001, *Cosmic Evolution: The rise of complexity in nature.*. Cambridge, MA, Harvard University Press.

Clouser, R., 1999, Is theism compatible with evolution. In Pennock, R.T. (Ed.) *Intelligent Design Creationism and its Critics*. Cambridge. MA, MIT Press, p. 511-536

Crick, F.H.C. 1997, *The Astonishing Hypothesis. The scientific search for the soul.* New York, Touchstone Books.

Dalrymple, G.B., 1991, *The Age of the Earth.* Stanford University Press.

Dawkins, R., 1976, *The Selfish Gene.* Oxford, Oxford University Press.

Dawkins, R., 1995, *River Out of Eden: A Darwinian View of Life.* New York, Harper Collins.

Dawkins, R., 2006, *The God Delusion.* New York, Bantam Press.

Delsemme, A.H., 1998, Cosmic Origin of the Biosphere. In Brack, A., (Ed.) *The Molecular Origins of Life. Assembling Pieces of the Puzzle.* New York, Cambridge University Press, 100-118.

DeMello, A., 1990, *Awareness: The Perils and Opportunities of Reality.* New York, Doubleday.

Dembski, W.A. (ed.), 1998, *Mere Creation: Science, Faith, and Intelligent Design.* Downers Grove, Ill, InterVarsity Press.

Dembski, W.A., 2002, *Detecting Design in the Natural Sciences.* Natural History, 111, 76.

Denison, M.,1956, *The Power to Go. The Story of the Automotive Industry.* Doubleday & Company, New York.

Dennett, D.C., 1991, *Consciousness Explained.* Little Brown and Company, New York.

Dennett, D.C., 2006, *Breaking the Spell. Religion as a Natural Phenomenon.* New York, Penguin Books.

Diamond, J., 1997, *Guns, Germs, and Steel. The fates of human societies.* New York, Norton.

Dodson, E., 1984, *The Phenomenon of Man Revisited.* New York, Columbia University Press.

Dowd, M., 2006, *Thank God for Evolution. How the marriage of science and religion will transform your life and our world.* New York, Viking.

Drury, S., 1999, *Stepping Stones. The Making of Our Home World,* Oxford, Oxford University Press.

Ellwood, G.F., 2001, *The Uttermost Deep. The Challenge of Near-Death Experiences.* New York, Lantern Books.

Futuyma,D.J., 1983, *Science on Trial. The Case for Evolution.* New York, Pantheon Books.

Gell-Mann, M., 1994, *The Quark and the Jaguar. Adventures in the Simple and the Complex.* New York, Freeman and Company.

Gibberson, K.W., 2008, *Saving Darwin. How to be a Christian and believe in evolution.* New York, Harper Collins.

Goswami, A., 1993, *The Self-Aware Universe: How consciousness Creates the Material World.* New York, Putnam.

Goswami, A., 2008, *Creative Evolution. A physicist's resolution between Darwinism and Intelligent Design.* Wheaton, Ill, Quest Books.

Gould, S.J., 1999, *Rocks of Ages. Science and Religion in the Fullness of Life.* New York, Ballantine Books.

Greenberg, A., 2000, *A Chemical History Tour, Picturing Chemistry from Alchemy to Modern Molecular Science.* New York, Wiley Interscience.

Harris, S., 2004, *The End of Faith. Religion, terror, and the future of reason.* New York, W.W. Norton and Company.

Haught, J.F., 2000, *God after Darwin, A Theology of Evolution.* Boulder, Westview Press.

Hixon, L., 1978, *Coming Home. The experience of enlightenment in sacred traditions.* Los Angeles, Jeremey Tarcher.

Hixon, L., 1992, *Great Swan, Meetings with Ramakrishna.* Boston, Shambhala.

Holland, H. D., 1994, Early Proterozoic atmospheric change. In *Early Life on Earth,* S. Bergston (ed.) Nobel Symposium 84, Columbia University Press, New York, pp.237-244.

Huxley, A.L., 1943, *The Perennial Philosophy.* New York, Harpers &

Brothers.

Johnson, P.E., 1991, *Darwin on Trial*. Downers Grove, Ill. InterVarsity Press.

Jones, R.H., 2008, *Science and Mysticism. A comparative study of western natural science,* Theravadan Buddhism and Advaita Vedanta. Bucknell University Press.

Kafatos, M. and Nadeau, R., 1990, *The Conscious Universe: The Scientific Truth of Psychic Phenomena*. New York, Springer-Verlag.

Kappelman, J., 1996, The evolution of body mass and relative brain size in fossil hominoids. *Journal of Human Evolution*. 30, 243-276.

Kauffman, S., 1995, *At home in the universe. The search the laws of self-organization and complexity*. New York, Oxford University Press.

Keating, T, 1995, Guidelines for Interreligious Understanding. Points of Agreement and Similarity. In Beversluis, J., (ed.) *A SourceBook for Earth's Community of Religions*. Grand Rapids, MI, CoNexus press. p.148.

Kelley, P. and Callanan, M., 1992, *Final Gifts. Understanding the special awareness, needs, and communications of the Dying*. New York, Simon & Schuster.

Kitchner, P., 2001, Born-again Creationism, In Pennock, R. T.,(ed) *Intelligent Design Creationism and its Critics,* Cambridge, Ma, MIT Press, 257-287.

Kuhn, T.S., 1962, *The Structure of Scientific Revolutions*. Chicago, University of Chicago Press.

Larson, E.J. and Witham, L., 1997, Scientists are still keeping the faith. *Nature*. 386, 435-436.

Larson, E.J. and Witham, L., 1998, Leading Scientists still reject God. *Nature* 394, 313.

Margulis, L., 1970, *The Origin of Eukaryotic Cells*. New Haven, Yale University Press.

McClenon, J., 2002, *Wondrous healing, Shamanism, Human*

Evolution and the Origin of Religion. Northern Illinois University Press, De Kalb, Ill.

Merton, T., 1972, *New Seeds of Contemplation.* New York, New Directions.

Miller, K.R., 1999, *Finding Darwin's God, A scientist's search for common ground between God and evolution.* New York, Cliff Street Books.

Miller, K.R., 2002, The Flaw in the Mousetrap, *Natural History.* 111, 75.

Miller, K.R., 2008, *Only a Theory. Evolution and the Battle for America's Soul.* New York, Viking Press.

Monod J. ,1972, *Chance and Necessity: An Essay on the Natural Philosophy of Modern Biology.* New York, Random House.

Moody, R.A., 1975, *Life after Life: The Investigation of a Phenomenon - Survival of Bodily Death.* New York, Bantam Books.

Morgan, C.L., 1927, *Emergent Evolution.* New York, Henry Holt.

Morris, H., 1985, *The Biblical Basis of Modern Science.* Grand Rapids MI, Baker Book House.

Morris, H.M. and Parker, G.E., 1982, *What is creation Science?* San Diego, Creation-Life publishers.

Morris, S.C., 2003, *Life's Solution. Inevitable humans in a lonely universe.* Cambridge, Cambridge University Press.

Newberg, A., D'Aquill, E., and Rause, B., 2001, *Why God Won't go Away: Brain Science and the Biology of Belief.* Ballantine Books, New York.

Noelle D.C., 2003, Searching for God in the machine. In Kurtz, P. (ed.) *Science and Religion, are they compatible?* Amherst New York, Prometheus Books, p 313-319.

Parker, S.T. and Gibson, K.R., 1979, A developmental model for the evolution of language and intelligence in early hominids. *Behavioral and Brain Science.* 2, 367-408.

Pennock, R.T., 1996, Naturalism, Evidence, and Creationism: The case of Phillip Johnson. *Biology and Philosophy.* 11, 543-549.

Pennock, R.T., 1999, *Tower of Babel: The Evidence against the New*

Creationism. Cambridge Mass, MIT Press.

Pennock, R.T., 2002, Mystery Science Theater, *Natural History,* 111, 77.

Plantinga, A., 1991, When faith and reason clash: Evolution and the Bible. *Christain Scholar's Review.* 21, 8-32.

Provine, W., 1988, Evolution and the Foundation of Ethics, *MBL Science.* 3, 25-29.

Ray, R.A., 2001, *Secret of the Vajra World: The Tantric Buddhism of Tibet.* Boston, Shambhala

Raymo, C., 1998, *Skeptics and True Believers. The Exhilarating Connection Between Science and Religion.* New York, Walker and Company.

Rolston, H.III, 1999, *Genes, Genesis, and God, Values and Their Origins in Natural and Human History.* Cambridge, Cambridge University Press.

Ruff, C.B., Trinkaus, E., and Holliday, T.W., 1997, *Body mass and encephalization in Pleistocene Homo.* Nature, 387, 173-176.

Ruse, M., 1982, *Darwinism Defended: A Guide to Evolutionary Controversies.* Reading Mass, Benjerman/Cummings Publication Company.

Ruse, M., 2001, *Can a Darwinian be a Christian? The relationship between science and religion.* Cambridge, Cambridge University Press.

Russell, B., 1961, What can a Free Man Worship, reprinted in B. Russell, 1972, *Atheism, Collected Essays 1943-1949.* New York, Arno Press.

Russell, M.J. and Hall, A. J., 1997, The emergence of life from iron monosulfide bubbles at a submarine hydrothermal redox and pH front. *Journal of the Geological Society of London.* 154. 377-402.

Rye, R. and Holland, H.D., 1998, Paleosols and the evolution of atmospheric oxygen: A critical review. *American Journal of Science,* 298, 621-672.

Scott, E.C., 2002, *The Nature of Change, Natural History.* 111, 79.

Scott, E.C. and Cole, H.P., 1985, The elusive scientific basis for creation 'science. *Quarterly Review of Biology.* 60, 21-30.

Seilacher, A., 1994, Early multicellular life: Late Proterozoic fossils and the Cambrian Explosion. In Bengtson, S (ed.) *Early life on Earth.* Nobel Symposium 84, Colombia University Press, New York, 389-400.

Smith, H., 1991, *The World's Religions: Our Great Wisdom Traditions.* San Francisco, Harper Collins.

Smith, H., 2001, *Why Religion Matters. The fate of the human spirit in an age of disbelief.* San Francisco, Harpers.

Smith, W., 1988, *Teilhardism and the New Religion,* Rockford Ill., Tan books

Stark R. and Finke R., 2000, *Acts of faith: Explaining the human side of religion.* Berkeley, University of California Press.

Stetter, K.O., 1998, Hyperthermophiles and their possible role as ancestors of modern life. In Brack, A., (ed.) *The Molecular Origins of Life. Assembling Pieces of the Puzzle.* New York, Cambridge University Press, 315-335.

Stringer, C., 2003, Out of Ethiopia, *Nature.* 423, 692-695.

Teasdale, W., 1999, *The Mystic Heart. Discovering a universal spirituality in the World's Religions.* Novato, Ca., New World Library.

Teilhard de Chardin, P., 1959, *The Phenomenon of Man.* New York, Harper & Row.

Thewissen, J.G.M. and Bajpai, S., 2001, Whale origins as a poster child for macroevolution. *Bioscience.* 51, 1017-1029.

Thewissen, J.G.M. and Williams, E.M., 2002, The early radiations of Cetades (Mammalia): Evolutionary Pattern and developmental correlations. *Annual Review of Ecology and Systematics.* 33, 73-90.

Towe, K., 1970, Oxygen-Collagen priority and the early metazoan fossil record. *Proceedings of the National. Academy of Sciences. USA* 65, 781-788.

Travisano, M., Mongold, J. A., Bennett, A.F., and Lenski, R.E.,

(1995) Experimental tests of the roles of adaptation, chance, and history in evolution. Science, 267, 87-90.

Van Till, H. J., 1991, When faith and reason cooperate. *Christian Scholars Review*. 21, 8-32.

Wells, J., 2002, Elusive Icons of Evolution, *Natural History*. 111, 78.

Wilber, K., 1995, *Sex, Ecology, Spirituality. The spirit of evolution.* Boston, Shambhala.

Wilber, K, 1998, *The Marriage of Sense and Soul: Integrating Science and Religion*. New York, Random House.

Wilber. K. 2006, *Integral Spirituality. A startling new role for religion in the modern and postmodern world.* Boston Mass, Integral Books.

Wills, C. and Bada, J., 2000, *The Spark of Life, Darwin and the Primeval Soup*. Cambridge, MA., Perseus Press.

Wilson, D.S., 2002, *Darwin's Cathedral, Evolution, Religion, and the Nature of Society.* Chicago, University of Chicago Press.

Wilson, E.O., 1998, *Consilience. The Unity of Knowledge*. New York, Vintage Books.

Wong, J.T.-F., Chen, J., Mat, W.-K., Ng, S.-K., Hong, X., 2007, Polyphasic evidence delineating the root of life and roots of biological domains. *Gene*. 403, 39-52.

Young, W., 1985, *The Fallacies of Creationism.* Calgary, Detselig

Zukov, G., 1979, *The Dancing Wu Li Masters: An Overview of the New Physics*. New York, Bantam New Age.